UYGHURLAND,
THE FARTHEST EXILE

Poems in this collection originally appeared in the following
books: *Uyghur Qizi Lerikisi* (1992) and *Roh Pesli* (1996), published by
Shinjang Yashlar-Osmurler Neshriyati (Urumqi, China); *Al-Soqout
Al-thaaniy* (1988), published by Al-Ahaly (Damascus, Syria); *Loghz
Al-A'araas* (1990), published by Al-Yanabia (Damascus, Syria);
Al-wasiy Ala Al-that (1997) and *Ka'an* (1998) published by Arward
(Tartous, Syria); *Fiy Atlaali Somar Haithu Oqiymu* (2003), published
by Al-Konouz Al-Adabiyyah (Beiruit, Lebanon); *Hessatiy Min Al-Lay*
(2007), published by the Ministry of Culture (Damascus, Syria).

Translations of some of these poems have previously
appeared in *Bengal Lights, Molossus, Two Lines: Landmarks*,
and *Two Lines: Some Kind of Beautiful Signal*.

ISBN: 978-1-9399419-11-8

Library of Congress Control Number: 2015932628

Cover design by Jaya Nicely; Cover photo by Stacey Irvin
Typeset by Scott Arany

Phoneme Media
1551 Colorado Blvd., Suite 201
Los Angeles, CA 90041

Phoneme Media is a nonprofit publishing and film production house, a
fiscally sponsored project of Pen Center USA, dedicated to disseminating
and promoting literature in translation through books and film.

www.phonememedia.org

UYGHURLAND,
THE FARTHEST EXILE

Selected Poems

Ahmatjan Osman

Translated from the Uyghur and Arabic
by Jeffrey Yang and Ahmatjan Osman

PHONEME
MEDIA
Los Angeles

CONTENTS

Translator's Preface

....

Eagle's nest empty...
Urumqi...
—Ahmatjan Osman

I first happened upon the work of Ahmatjan Osman in 2009 while editing a folio on Uyghur poetry for the annual anthology of world literature *Two Lines #17: Some Kind of Beautiful Signal.* Looking for anything written about Uyghur literature at the college library near my home, I found a translated fragment of Osman's poem "Robinson Crusoe" quoted in a scholarly paper by Michael Friederich. Osman writes: *I will watch everything / through doubtful eyes / I am the Robinson of the times / I will build my island / on the other side / of the world.* By a fortunate coincidence, my co-editor of the folio, the founding director of Radio Free Asia Uyghur Service, Dolkun Kamberi, had known Osman when he was still living in Syria and in 2004 had helped him and his family find asylum in Canada. Kamberi, who serves as one of the few current news information conduits between Uyghurs living in a brutally oppressed East Turkistan (Xinjiang province) and the outside world, passed me Osman's telephone number.

When I phoned Osman, a quiet female voice answered. I asked for Ahmatjan Osman and the voice turned suspicious, quickly asking who I was and what I wanted. After my reply, without warning another anxious female voice replaced the first and fired more questions at me. Then a moment of silence on the line as I awaited the flames of a third trial, but instead a voice claiming to be Osman materialized. That conversation would mark the beginning of our collaboration: over the next four years Osman would send me a kind of skeleton key in English of his original Uyghur and Arabic poems, which I would further distort (not knowing either language) and send back to him along with a list of detailed questions, which he would reply to, and back and forth we've slowly proceeded despite my ignorance.

It should go without saying that a translator's base-level responsibility is to know the language of the original. However, as we weren't able to find someone who knew not only Uyghur and Arabic but also American poetry, and as there is some remarkable historical precedence for good, if not exceptional, translations rendered under the guidance of a knowledgeable informant, we pressed on. This was most fortunate for me as engaging with Osman's work at this micro-level has opened up a totally new and fascinating poetic-cultural space in my mind. On more than a few occasions, too, Osman has quelled my emails of despair with replies of ebullience and surprise upon seeing an overdraft (to borrow Basil Bunting's word for translation). Let sympathetic readers judge.

Ahmatjan Osman was born into a Muslim Uyghur family in 1964 in Urumqi. His father managed a coal mine and during the Cultural Revolution was accused of being a "bourgeoisie capitalist" and sentenced to six years of "reform through hard labor" at a penal camp. "For this reason," Osman says, "I grew up feeling like I was the son of someone guilty of a crime, as other children often teased me about my father." After spending many years in and out of the hospital for lung disease, his father died when Osman was eighteen. Osman's mother took care of the household, which included her three children. Her spirit, the spirit of the stories she told Osman as a child, of the folk poetry she sang to him from memory, were an important influence on Osman's work.

When Osman was thirteen, he sent three poems to a radio station in Urumqi and they were read on the air. This marked his first publication. Besides Uyghur folk poetry, early literary influences Osman acknowledges include collections of Tang poetry, Lao Zi, early nineteenth century English and Russian Romantic poetry, as well as essays by the literary critic Vissarion Grigoryevich Belinsky—the originator of the Russian school of social realism in the 1840s. The Uyghur poets of a previous generation, Qurban Barat and Boghda Abddulla, were also significant for him, as well as the Chinese *menglong* (朦朧, "misty/hazy/obscure") poets, such as Bei Dao, Gu Cheng, Duo Duo, Mang Ke, among others. In Urumqi at that time, very few books were available in Uyghur translation, and it wasn't until he received a scholarship to study Arabic literature at the University of Damascus that Osman immersed himself in foreign literature. While at university, Osman became one of the central figures of what came to be known as the new poetry movement, or *gungga*, that emerged around the popular literary magazine in Urumqi, *Tangritagh* (天山, Tian Shan, "Heavenly Mountains": the name of a network of mountain ranges in Central Asia, Urumqi being situated at its eastern base. *Tangri*, or *tengri*, also refers to the Sky God, the chief deity of the pre-Islamic Tengrism religion.) *Gungga*, a direct translation of the Chinese *menglong*, absorbed the vision and aesthetic principles of that groundbreaking movement though its literary manifestations were necessarily different. According to Osman and the editor of *Tangritagh* Ablikim Baqi, who for several years now has worked with Dolkun Kamberi at Radio Free Asia, *gungga* demonstrated an opening out of traditional form and content, an art unfettered by any implicit message of "social value," and offered a new vision of Uyghur poetry as attuned to the French symbolists Baudelaire and Mallarmé, the surrealists Breton and Aragon, as well as to Manichaean scripture and the Sufi poets Shah Meshrep and Ali-Shir Nava'i. *Tangritagh* published many translations of foreign poets as well as the work of Osman and other Uyghur poets such as Batur Rozi, Parhat Tursun, and Arkin Nur. Its first issue was published in 1986 and it continues to this day.

After college, in the late eighties and early nineties, Osman worked as a journalist in Urumqi while continuing to write and publish poetry in magazines and newspapers. He translated the work of Jalal ad-Din Rumi, Fernando Pessoa, Paul Celan, Octavio Paz, and Adonis—an early admirer of Osman's poetry—into Uyghur. As a poet he writes in both Uyghur and Arabic, though due to political pressure, as it became increasingly difficult for him to publish in Uyghur in Xinjiang, he turned mostly to Arabic, even translating some of his own Uyghur poems into the other language. To note one example of Osman's writing practice, his poem "Dwelling in the Warmth of Other Moons" was written in both Uyghur and Arabic over a four-year period during his college years. Such a polyglossic existence has been a historic norm for many writers forced into exile—displaced from place, culture, language: home. As Osman became more publicly prominent as a poet and journalist, and due to his connections to Uyghur organizations overseas, the Chinese authorities intensified their cycle of harassment, arrest, imprisonment, and release. He moved to Syria in 1994 with his family, and in 2004, under pressure from the Chinese government (though his wife is a Syrian national), he was deported to Canada. He has resided there ever since, finding work in a grocery store, a coffee factory, and currently, in a warehouse as a forklift operator. In the afternoon of the first day of a three-day conference Osman organized on the East Turkistan National Movement in September 2014—after a day of talks and discussions among writers, politicians, activists, journalists, and lawyers—participants marched from the hotel lobby where the conference was being held to a demonstration in front of the Chinese Consulate-General. *Uyghurland, the Farthest Exile* is Osman's first poetry collection to appear in English, and as far as I know, the first book by a Uyghur poet to be published in English translation.

*

My deep thanks to Ahmatjan Osman, Dolkun Kamberi, Anna Rosenwong, Olivia Sears and CJ Evans at the Center for the Art of Translation, and David Shook and Christopher Heiser at Phoneme—pages raised to love's labor.

—Jeffrey Yang

Author's Preface

Traditional Uyghur poetry is rooted in shamanism and animism, and poetic inspiration is understood as an actual presence, what is unseen, which speaks through the poet. The speaker of the poem is an inspired other that is not the poet, for the poet exists simply as a vessel for the lyric voice, which assumes the nature of a sanctified being. Poetry is thus sanctification, and the poet a messenger between the sacred unseen and the listener-reader.

The Uyghur poet summons an unknown presence in the absence felt by the living.

Connecting this ancient role of verse to contemporary Uyghur poetry, one can turn to Roland Barthes' idea of the death of the author. For Barthes, the poet is essentially a copyist of a text written by an anonymous author who originates in the unknown. Heidegger describes this phenomenon in a different way when he says that the poet is one who listens to language speak for us in what is spoken.

The Uyghur poet listens to the absence that inspires speech.

Mallarmé defines this poetic language as a gift from the gods, or chance, as recorded by poets across the ages to today. Rimbaud famously said, "I is another."

I, too, am one of the many.

—Ahmatjan Osman

السقوط الثاني

from

THE SECOND FALL

(1988)

ئەگىملەر

بۆلۈم ئەگىمسى

مەن جىرسىپ كەتمەي دەپ سېنى يىگىلايمەن ،
تېنىڭ بىلەن روھ ئارا ھەيران بولغان ھالدا تۇرىمەن.
ھەربىكەتنى تۇتىمەن ،
ساڭا ئۆلىنىمەن ،
تېنىمنىڭ پارچىلىرى تەگگە چۈشۈپ كېتىدۇ.
سېنى ئۆلتۈرىمەن ،
ئەسلىك قېنىمدىن چىقىدۇ.
سېنى ئۇدراكتا تۇرغۇزىمەن ،
تۆرەلمىلەرنى تىتىپ ،
يۈزۈمگە سېبكونتلاردەك چاچىسەن.
بىر قىتىم ، سېنى شەبنەمنىڭ ھۆسىسىزلقىدا كۆرۈپ قالدىم ،
جەۋھەرىڭگى ئويناۋاتاتتىڭ ،
ئۆنى سەھندىن ئايرىۋاتاتتىڭ ،
ئۆنى ۋەقەنىڭ زۆلمىتىدە ينتترسىپ قويۋاتاتتىڭ ،
توزىۋاتاتتىڭ.
سېنى تۆيىمەن ،
مەندە غايىب بولسەن ،
سېنى بولسۇن دەپ سېنى ساڭا سۆرەيمەن.
ھەرپىلەردىن ئۆتكىن دەپ سەندىن ئۆتىنىمەن ،
سەن پارتلاپ كېتىسەن ،
ھەرپىلەر ھورغا ئايلىنىپ كېتىدۇ.
تېنىڭ بىلەن روھ ئارا ھەيران بولغان ھالدا تۇرىمەن ،
سېنى زاۋال تاپمىسۇن دەپ ساڭا مۇھتاج بولىمەن ،
بولمىسا مەنمۇ زاۋال تاپىمەن

Arcs

Arc of Being

I recreate you so as not to rot
I stand bewildered between your soul and body
I touch something moving
I touch you
and my limbs drop into the depths
I sacrifice you
and your origins spill from my blood
I trap you with perception
you fragment the fetuses
casting them across my face as seconds
I saw you once in a dew-soaked dream
danced with your essence
that separated from you
and faded into the darkness
When I perceive you
you disappear in me
I drag you toward your self to be
I beg you to cross over the words
and you explode
the letters evaporate
I stand bewildered between your body and soul
I need you not to vanish to keep me from vanishing

بۇ ماڭا قانداقلارچه يۈز بېردۇ ،

قانداقلارچه يۈز بېردۇ...

تۇساتتىن سېنىڭ خاتىرجەم ئۆزلۈكۈڭنى تۇتقانلىقىمنى كۆرمەن-دە ،

چۈشۈپ كېتىسەن ، چۈشۈپ كېتىمەن ،

ھېچنېمىدىن بولغان بىر كاللەكتەك چۈشۈپ كېتىمىز.

تەنھالىق ئەگمىسى

شام ئۆزىنىڭ بالبىق خامخىيالىنى سۈرسۇن ، مەيلى ،

كېچەلەر كەينى-كەينىدىن كۈندۈزنىڭ كۆلچىكىگە چۈشۈپ كەتسۇن ، مەيلى.

سېنىڭ پۈخراالرى يوق بۇ تەختتىن

ھەمدە تەگرىڭنىڭ يۈزىددەك يېشىللىشىشۋاتقان بۇ سەرلىق تاياقتىن باشقا ھېچنېمەك يوق.

كىمنىڭ مىراسخورىسەن ؟

نېمىدىن ئۆچ ئالماقچىسەن ؟

دېگىزنىڭ خىلۋەتچىلىك ئۈستىكەنى قانداقمۇ قايتىتۈرۈپ بېرەلەرسەن ؟!

چاقچۇقنىڭ ئۆلۈكلەر بويىقىدىن ۋاز كېچىشى

ھەمدە مىسنىڭ قىرغىنچىلىق قىرغاقلىرىدا تېپىلىپ كېتىشى چوقۇم.

سۈ ۋاستە بولماي قالدى ،

مانا بۇ قورامتاشلارنىڭ شەرنىسى نۇر ھەيكەلىدەك يىقىلدى.

ھېچكىم ئۇلجىۋا قارشى چىك تۆرۈۋاتقان خاتىرجەمتا ئەمەس ،

خۇددى بۇ ئۈشنىڭ ئۆزىنىڭ بىلەن ئاللاقسى يوقتەك ،

خۇددى ئاپەتنىڭ ھەجمى ئۆنى تۈنجى رەت قورقىتىۋاتقاندەك.

چۈغلىنىپ كەتكەن چۈشنىڭ يىراقلىقلىرىدا مانا مۈشۈنداق قېقىلىپ-سوقۇلۇپ يۈرىسەن ،

يوقلۇقنىڭ قاتتىقلىقىدىن زارلىنىپ ،

تۈنجى بېخىنىڭ نەسلىنى كېچىنىڭ ئاخىرىغىچە كۈشەپ.

4

How is this happening to me?
How is this happening. . . ?
I feel the unexpected touch of your solid self—
you fall and so do I. . .
We fall as a cluster of nothingness

Arc of Isolation

Let the candle live its childish illusion
let the boats fall apart   one by one   in the basin of the day
You own nothing but a throne without citizens
and a pale green scepter like the face of God
Whom are you heir to?
For what do you avenge yourself?
How can you give the sea back its wish for isolation?
Fired clay abandons the casts of the dead
copper slides along the outskirts of the massacre
water is no longer a way. . .
Here the rocks' sap drips into a structure of light
No one's at ease with the stability formed against prey
as if it doesn't concern them
as if for the first time afraid of the disaster's magnitude
So you wander through an accretion of dreams
complain about the solidity of nothingness
reflect on the offspring of the first germ
until night's end

كېسىلگەن باش ئەگمىسى

ئەمدى سۆكۈتمگدىن يالىڭاچلانغان ھالدا تۇرسەن ،
بوشلۇق سىنى بۇرۇنقىدەك ئۆز ئىچىگە ئالمىغان ،
ھەمدە ئەسنىك ھەۋەس جىرنىڭى قالمىغان.
تورلىرىڭنى سىياھتىن يىغىپ باق ،
كېسىلگەن بىشىڭنى ئاڭا ئىلقىلق ھالدا كۆرسەن.
ئەي ، كەپسىز ، نەگە بېرىپ توختتدىڭ ؟
ھەرپىلەرنىڭ سىرى تېخى تۈگمىدىمۇ يە ؟!
بەلكىم دېرىزە بىر دەمدىن كېيىن ئۆمۈچۈككە ئايلىنىپ قالدۇ-دە ،
ساراڭلىقنىڭ ئۆچۈشتىن باشقا شەھۇتى قالمايدۇ.
ئەي ، مونولوگ ، ئىلگىرىلە ،
چوۋۇلۇش زاماندا بىلگۈنى رۇسلا.
ئەمدى ، خىيانەت يولتۇزى چاقنىغانىدىن كېيىن ،
رەت قىلىش ئىنچىلىنىڭ نېمە پايدىسى ؟!
ھەققەت دېگەن ساھىلنىڭ قول پۇلاڭلىتىشى ،
خامخىياللىق كېمەك بىلەن يىراقلاپ كەت.

سۆرگۈنگاھ ئەگمىسى

بۇ يەر
ھەم ئۇ يەردە ،
لەڭگەرگە كۆرۈنۈپ تۇرغان بايرام يوق.
بۇ يەر ھەم ئۇ يەردە ،
پەقەت
بىر دېڭىز قاراقچىسىنىڭ ناخشسى
ھەم كەلكۈننىڭ ئۇستىگە ئۆرلىگەن ئاياللىق
نىڭ تەپسىلاتىدىن سىرت
خەتەر دەپ ئاتاشقان غايىپ نەرسىلا بار.

Arc of the Severed Head

You now stand naked in silence
no emptiness contains you as it once did
memory without a note of longing
Pull your net from the ink
and see your severed head waiting
O wretched man, where did you find your end?
Or do the words' letters still contain their secrets?
The window might become a spider in time
and what remains for madness is but extinction's desire
Go ahead, Monologue!
Be patient in the moment of disintegration
What is the use of the gospel of rejection
now with the star of betrayal ablaze?
The truth is the crash of a wave on the beach—
go away, depart in your imaginary boat

Arc of Exile

Here
and there
no harbor overlooks the ritual
Everything here and there
is the absence they call danger
with no details of a pirate's song
nor of femininity before the flood

بۇ يەر ھەم ئۇ يەردە ،
ساڭا بىر چاقماق ھەققىدە سۆز قىلىشماقتا ،
دېگىنكى: يۇرتلارنىڭ ھىدىنى كۆتۈرۈپ يۈرۈشكەن پاقلار يوق ،
سۆرگۈنگاھتۇر بۇ
دولقۇنلارنىڭ تۇمشۇقلىرى يۆتكەپ تۇرغان.

ئۇمىدسىزلىك ئەگمىسى

بۇقىلارنىڭ شادلىقىقفا ئىچكىرىلەپ كىرگەن بىر سەھەردە ،
ئايال قىرغاقلاردىن نىجاتلىق تىلىمىگەندە ،
ھەمدە قىرغاقلاردا
دەرىزە
ياكى ئۇنتۇلغان سايە بولمىغاندا ،
شۇندىاقلا ، تۇرمۇش شامالالرغا قەرزدار بولمىغاندا...
قاراڭغۇ روھتىن ئەسنەپ چىقىسەن.

ئۆگزە ئەگمىسى

سەزگۈنىڭ ئۇيقۇقسىمان قۇشى ،
پۈتلىرى بىر-بىرىگە قارشى تارىخ ،
ئاتەشنىڭ مۇراسىملىرى ،
كىرىستلەر ،
ھەيكەللەر ،
تەرەپلەرنىڭ بىر ئەمچەككە باش قويۇشى ،
بارماقلار ئۆگزىلەرنى تۇتقان يەردە.

Here and there
they tell you about a flash of lightning
So reply, No frogs bear the smell of a country
it is exile
that the beaks upon the waves circulate

Arc of Despair

One morning, from deep beneath the bull's joy
when no woman seeks the help of the shore
and will not be a window onto the shore
nor a forgotten shadow
and to live isn't to owe the wind...
you will emerge from the dark spirit
yawning

Arc of the Surface

A bird perpendicular to earth
A history of conflicts
Rituals of fire
Crosses
Statues
Slumber of distances beneath the breast
where the fingers touch the surface

ھەيرانلىق ئەگمسى

مىجىكىم قاپتاللار بۆرسىسگە ھەمراھ بولىمدى...
ئاۋۇ قىبىپ كەتكەن ساھەدە سەن يالغۇز ،
ئەي ، تۆيغۇ داستىخىنىندا بوغۇزلىنىۋاتقان بۇقنىڭ ھەيرانلىقى ئىجرە
ئۇزاق ۋاقىت سۆرگۈچى !

ئەركنلىك ئەگمسى

قانىدىن ياسالغان ھاسسفا تايانغان
تۆغۈت ئانسى
ھەم يەرلىككە قويىغۇچى.

ھاۋا ئەگمسى

ئۇنىڭ ئەكس ئېتىش ئىقتىدارى يوق ،
ئۇ يۆكسەك شەكىلنىڭ يانتۇلۇقنى يارىتىدۇ.
ئۇ ھاۋا تىبكىستىگە يول ئاچقۇچى...
ئۇ ئۇزننىڭ توختاۋسىز ئىپقىنىدا قىسقارتىلىشقا بەرداشلىق بېرەلمەيدۇ.
ئۇ ھەۋەستەك سىرلىق ،
شامالدەك سەرسان ،
ئۇ خۇددى ئىچىمىزدە پاناھلانغان سۇدەك

Arc of Astonishment

No one amused the wolf on the slope
You are alone in the strange field
You who stare so long
in astonishment at the bull being slaughtered
on the table of speculation

Arc of Freedom

The midwife
the gravedigger
with a crutch of blood

Arc of Air

Irreversible
I form the descent of the higher figure
I open the space for a text of air
unable to cut off my streaming progression
Ambiguous as desire
unpredictable as the wind
refugee water in all of us

وهم البياض

ماذا نفعل بهذا العالم؟
الجمال واقف أمام جسر يتدهور ،
شبح جديد يلبس البهجة
ويرتفع من الهاوية.
بشر يتقمصون جسد كتابة
عن خاتمة الأمجاد على لوح الفناء.
الكلمة لا تحبل إلا بالحس ،
والحزن ميت يطلب الدفن.
ما تبقَّى من الزمان
هو الرنين المشتعل على تاج الملك المخلوع.
هات أغنية تثقب النهار
كي يهرب النصر
إلى الخيال المستعد للعبور
في نهر اللا موجود.

للشوارع
انحناءات شموع لقامة الفولاذ.
وحداثة لشهواتنا
لا تخرج إلى المروج
قبلما تعود إلى الحظيرة الدروب.
وراء للوراء ،
وأمام بين ضوضائنا
يتسرب من قربان نعده لما يأتي ولمن...
نسكن برج الأيام ،
ونثقب الجدران
بحثاً عن لحظة تحرسها القطط الحكيمة.
ثم نبقى نتساءل:

The Illusion of Whiteness

What shall we do with this world?
Beauty stands before a decrepit bridge
while a new specter draped with delight
rises from the abyss
Humans incarnate in writing
the end of glory on the chessboard of dissolution
Words no longer pregnant but in sensation
sadness passes away, requests a burial
What remains of time
is the burning reign of the deposed king's crown
Reader, lend me a song that bears the day
for the victory to escape
for vigilant imagination to cross
the river to nonexistence

The streets curve with candles
against a structure of steel
Our modernized desires
do not leave the path for the meadow
on the way back to the barn
Back, further back,
and ahead the noise
between us leaks out
from the oblations we prepare for arrival
We dwell in a tower of days
climb the walls
in search of the moment once guarded

كيف يخرج الخنزير من أدغال الزمن
ويقتحم غير آمالنا؟!
لا تنتظر أكثر ،

اخرجْ أيها العمق.
أعرف أنك لا تجيد الوقوف
على رقعة الشطرنج.
لقد مات الملوك ،
والقلاع خاوية من سهام مصقولة
في بلاد ما وراء الذات.
إنها حكمة البشر
تنهق في الكواليس.
وأرجوحة للتمثال
مصنوعة من الأحصنة ومسامير الذهن.
أنصتْ جيداً:
أليست ارتعاشة الأعشاب النابتة في العواء
تقضمها الأرانب؟!

من يخطف الغياب من بيننا ،
ومن يتدحرج أصله فوق أجسادنا ،
ثم من الذي ينفصل
يتصل ،
ينحدر من ظلال تندلف إلينا؟!
أما آن للوقت أن ينصب خيمته
على تاج الأمكنة
ويترك الغرائز ترعى في الكلأ
المنبثق
من جوهرنا؟
لماذا نمد هذا العذاب

by the wisdom of cats
Instead we are left to wonder
how the wild boar released from time's forest
destroys everything but our hopes

Do not wait anymore
Depart into the abyss
I don't know how
to stand upon this chessboard
Kings die
and castles emptied of arrows
are polished in a country without self-knowledge
The wisdom of humanity
echoes in the ideal
a statue of a horse nailed in the mind
Listen closely, Reader,
to the rabbits eating
the young shoots in the meadow

Who steals the inner distance from us?
Tumbles over our bodies
and divides
the shadows within us?
We must let time
set up its tent upon the crown of a place
where instinct can graze on the pasture
from which our essence grows
Why must we extend suffering
to others?

إلى الضفة الأخرى ؟
حيث الزمن يغفو
والجسد لا يحمل الثمار
والأزهار المفترسة تندلع
من فم الأسطورة اليانعة .
هكذا يفجؤنا الغريب ،
غير عابئ بثرثرة الرعب وشرعة النسق ،
لا يفصل من أذهاننا
غير المرغوب فيه
غير المغضوب عليه
ويتركه في متاهات ما ظننّا أنه يجيء .
حتام نبقى ندور
بين الأصل والنقيض ،
ألكي نصل إلى البداية المهجورة ؟!
ومَن الثالث
خارج الأصل ،
خارج النقيض !

هوذا يطلع من شكله الشكل
عارياً إلا من خيانة الرحم ،
موزعاً بين لحظة اغتراب الخطى
وانتصاب الظلال فوق المراسي .
أيهذا الواقف في برج الفراغ ،
في أي رغبة رأيت السحيق يعشّش ؟
ها هي الدروب آخذة شكل الثعابين
في مخيلة الغبار ،
وينهض الشفاف متأملاً أجزاءه اللامرئية .
هل توهمت شيئاً يا أيها البياض ،
يا صمت الصاخبين على ضفاف الحلم ،

When time sleeps
the body doesn't bear fruit
wild flowers rot in the mouth
We are astonished
by the extraordinary
and indifferent to the horrors and the prearranged contracts
We cannot separate ourselves from the mind
but what we desire, what we despise
remains separate in the maze of the imagined future
Do we move
between the origin and its opposition
so as to return to the abandoned beginning?
Or is there a third possibility
beyond the dialectic of origins
and oppositions?

Form rises from form
bare of any content that recalls the womb
torn between the estranged step
and the light lengthening across the harbor
You, standing in the tower of emptiness,
can you see the nest of timeless desire?
The path of snakes into the unexpected
imagination's dust—
transparency, the contemplation of parts unseen
Whiteness, what do you want?
Silent measure on the shores of dream
Womb deep within another womb
Is there no one here at the coronation?

يا جنيناً موغلاً في الجنين ؟

من سواك يجتاح هذا التتويج ؟

من سواك نتفتح في رحمه ونحيا ؟

من سواك ... ؟

أسأل الدهشة عن ذاكرة المنحني إلى حتفه ،

وأحدّث الغروب عن التدفق العنيف.

فليمض الزمن بلا زمن

أو ليرسُ في شاطئنا المزدحم.

لا فرق بين الموت والموت

إلا باشتعاله في أقنعة النصر.

Is there no one here reborn?
Is there no one. . . ?
I ask after the one whose memory bowed to his death
to the flow of violence spoken at sunset
If time could pass without time
anchor near our overcrowded beach
and between one death and another
death, the difference ignited by a mask of victory

لغز الأعراس

from

The Mystery of Weddings

(1990)

نشيد البدء

من ينهض كلحن العزاء من الرقاد الشامل ؟
من الذاهب فجأة إلى بزوغ البحر في هذا الليل
مستسلماً لعذوبة الجسد
لصراخ الزهرة الحيرى
مترهفاً لاخضرار الذهب الخالص
وهو يرتطم في الروح ؟

أنا ما رأيت النور يهذي على شاطئ السر
أنا ما قصدت أن لعمقي الداجي
حدس الموت صادحاً في الصباح
أخذني هودج العزة من سكرة الألم
مترثئاً بصمتي
أم تمجيداً لي ؟!
لكني أتهادى على المروج الذاهبة إلى غموض الشمس
وفي تاجي المنتشي يزهو جحيمي
مرتدياً قناعي المشكوك فيه
متحلياً بدم الطاووس
أمتدح لغزك المشرق يا ملاك الأعراس

Ode of Commencement

Who rises in a melody of solace
from the depths of sleep?
Who escapes the night like quicksilver
and emerges from the sea
in surrender to the body's delights
the screaming of a bewildered flower
who hears the greening of gold purity
pour into the soul?

I have not seen the light murmur
on the secret shore
nor can the darkness within me
predict the death warbles of morning

Was it pride that brought me upon a camel howdah
from suffering to compassion
all for my own glorification?
I who tremble with ecstasy in the meadows
hidden from the sun
my rapturous crown, depths of hell
I wear my mask of doubts
adorned with the blood of the peacock
and praise your bright mystery
O angel of weddings

تاج في اللهب

ما دام قد أشرفت الكارثة الكبرى
ما دام قد لفنا كل هذا الخمول
في هذا المكان
فأكيد هو الحضور الثقيل للمتعة
وأكيد هو الغناء
ها هوذا طعم المرارة في أعيننا
ظل شاسع من الخفافيش إذ يرف
كم هو شاحب هذا الصباح
إذ يعلو أسطحتنا
وكم هو واهن صوت الطبول
مجدبة هي الكروم
فعلى النافذة يحتضر النشيد
وظامئات إلى النشوة نساؤنا الكابيات...

أيها الإنسان
يا عناء الزهرة في الصخور
يا شقاء عامراً بالقبلة ورنين الثلاثين من الفضة...
كن على يقين من غراب الجوع
في جوف التراب
فثمة وشاح من الرؤى
يسدله على الشمس عنكبوت الأنواء
فجأة يندلع الرماد
ذلك الكاهن المشؤوم ريح الأوثان
ويجرف كل مراكبنا المهشمات إلى شطآن القحط
مستنفداً فينا البروق العطشى وهدير الغابات

24

A Crown in the Flame

As long as the final disaster nears
as long as the indifference surrounds us here
the boredom of pleasure is as certain
as a song
The bitterness in our eyes
is a vast shadow of bats in flight
How pale the morning wakes
the surfaces of our homes
how weak the beating of drums
The vineyards are dried
the ode extinguished in the window
women thirst for ecstasy

O humanity
O suffering flower among the rocks
O misery full of kisses and the clinking
of thirty silver pieces. . .
Is the crow's hunger deep underground
in the weave of dream
a storm of spiders blocks the sun

Ash pours out
the priest's forebodings
wind of idolatry sweeps our smashed boats
onto abandoned beaches
exhausts the lightning's thirst and the roars of the forest

والسكون آه السكون

يا سكون منتصف الليل

أيها الفجر البعيد والمثقل بناقوس الهجران...

ها هي ذي الشمس العظيمة

والذهب المتوهج في النيران

إذ تعبر فوقه طير الظلام

والجراد الحائم حول النبع

وخديعة الثعبان الذي يستريح عند جذع السنديان

وأصوات الصقور التي تعلو

وتربك الخراف وألحان الراعي

والبكاء القديم والأليف دوماً بالبهجة الغامضة...

كل ذلك يرقد بسلام في أغواري

اشتعلي أيتها السماء الآبدة

وانبثقي أيتها الأجراس

لا وقوفاً عند النور بل مستحيل

إن في عينيّ من رقص البحار وخفقان الأسرار

ما ليس يدركه النور

حي هو كل شيء إذ يموت كل شيء

في وطني يا كهفي العريق إيه يا صمتي

فيا لجفون تحتمل كل هذا الأفول وتزهو...

إنه لحكمة مدهشة متناهية الكمال

وجودك بيننا على هذه الأرض أيها الحلم

يا سهماً بهيئة الحمام

أطلقه قوس عتيد يدعى الأزل

يا نجمة أسمى عند ذروة القوس

Stillness, ah stillness!
O the stillness of midnight
O the distant dawn
heavy with the gong of desertion. . .
Gold glows in the fire
of the sun's expanse
as dark birds cross overhead
grasshoppers swirl around the wellspring
the serpent's deception
rests in the trunk of the old oak
hawks soar with shrieks
that disturb the sheep and the songs of the shepherd
the ancient cry a familiar, mysterious joy
deep within me, peace

Burn eternal heaven!
Come out with the bells!
Do not stand in the impossible light
in my eyes
waves dance on a secret sea
the light cannot illuminate
Everything is alive   everything dies
my home   my prehistoric cave   my silence
Blessed are the eyelids that seal all decline and pride
the amazement and absolute wisdom
of our being on this earth

القوس الأشبه بالساقَين

يا موعد الدم

يا نمرأ يحيى في تفاصيل البحر

يا سمّال العيون

يا ضوء الكلام

يا خلود التاج في اللهب

يا أيها الفناء المحتدم

O dream
O arrow in the shape of a pigeon
shot by a bow called eternity
O highest star at the bow's peak
between the folds of a woman
O day of blood
O tiger living in the figures of sea
O darkening sight
O luminous words
O immortal crown in the flame
and the glowing dissolution

مينرفا، يا صخب الغياب

هذه السنابل حلم مقدس
كنت تنسجينه بخبث مريع
نعمتك المستردة من
فردوسك المفقود أيتها الخادمة
حارسك الوفي لمباهج المخدع
لها لون بشرتنا وطعم العذاب

أنت الرأس المتدلي من شباكنا العالي
يا لهول التحول
تقرعين ناقوس الفيضان
خلف جماجمنا الفائقة البروز كحزن البغال...
ها نحن نكون الآن كما لم نكن
سلمنا الأمانة الخبّأتها لأجلنا
في قصر أبيك الشامخ بين الحراس الصارمين

أيتها العرافة
يا لؤلؤة تصدح في الزبد...
كنت تعلمين حدوث المعجزة العظمى
حين تتحلل الأشياء المفضلة
تحت أجراس الرحيل
ويهبط الفجر الأمثل
على هضاب صدورنا المتدرجة إلى تاجك التام الاكتمال
يا ثمرة متأزمة لموسم اللحظة
عندما تحيكين لنا موتاً
أمكيدة كنت تأملين لخدعة الزمان
أم حبنا لك قد أضرم فينا شعلة الفناء

Minerva, O the Noise of Absence

To Norma

The wheat spikes are a holy dream
you reap with such malice
They are your benediction, servant
as existence is to the poets
recovered from your lost paradise
loyal guards to your chamber's delights
the flesh-tinged taste of suffering

Your head hangs down from the high window
of perfection, in death
With such horror
you sound the bell of the flood
behind our prominent skull, the sadness
of a mule within
We are here now as we were not before
as poets, give us the treasure that you hid from us
in your father's infinite palace
safeguarded with vigilance

O sibyl
O pearl warbling in the foam
You recognize the miracle that takes place
when precious ideals fail
beneath the bells of departure
dawn rises over the hills
enters the body bowed
toward the resplendent crown

حتى تبدّى لنا شخصك
تلك الزهرة الأزلية ؟
هل اغتصابك أعراسنا أيتها الكاذبة
يا عروس الخلود
يا عقرباً يفيض بالرحمة
يا لون العذاب الزاهي
لك أمجادنا
لك جميع أسرّتنا الشامخة
كصرخة امرأة في سكون الليل
أشرعتنا لك والبحار والغنيمة الكبرى
سننصب لك هياكل الذهب في ساحات المدينة
سنحرق لك أقنعتنا والبخور
لك مذبحنا عند أعالي النهار ...

أبتها الممجَّدة
الأكثر سخطاً بالقرابين
إنها الدورة الأبدية لرحمك الأكثر طغياناً
ضحاياها نحن في حضورنا العابث والثقيل
كذلك يخطفنا حتم الاحتدام في اللذة الغائمة
على حين غرة
في لحظة ترسم دوائر من الكينونة أرحب فأرحب ...
حيث الساق تسبح في الهواء
على بعد عن الساق
والقهر يلج بتشكك عظيم في الغياب الجميل

انهضي بهالة مائنا في رياحك القادمة
يا واهبة البيان الموهوبة بآفة الخرس
وامنحينا خاتم الزواج
ضعي في أصابعنا الأكثر موهبة

O seasons' fruits of crisis
when you spun death in us
did you think you could trick time?
Or did our love for you kindle our dissolution
until you seemed
an undying flower?
And to rape you becomes a wedding?
O liar
O bride of immortality
O scorpion that overflows with mercy
O rich color of suffering

Our glories are for you
from the towering beds
the screams of women in the still night
are for you
Our sails are for you
and the seas . . . and the final prize!
For you we raise gold statues in town squares
we burn our masks and light incense for you
build an altar for you in the apex of days

O glorified one
so discontent with gifts
In the eternal cycle of your tyrannical womb
we are your victims, an absurd presence
The anticipated glow of pleasure-filled clouds
casts its spell
while the moment

بتحريك أحجار على رقعة السر
خاتمَك المصنوع من ذهب القُبلة
أيتها الزوجة الأكيدة
يا إشراقة الصمت
يا لغز الكلام

draws circles of being that ripple out
Legs kick the air, each disconnected from the other
Oppression penetrates the beautiful absence
with deep uncertainty

Rising with the halo of spent water
your wind surges
mute existence letting us speak
Give us the wedding ring
so that we might approach the unknown
and move the pieces on the chessboard of mystery
Your ring that is made of a golden kiss
O bound wife
O bright silence
O enigmatic words

ئۇيغۇر قىزى لەرىكسى

from

ODE TO A UYGHUR GIRL

(1992)

روبىنسون كروزو

I

چىقتىم كېپەك
ۋۇجۇدۇمدىن ئەكس سادا ئىدى.
چاقاي ئەمدى بارچە ئەينەكنى ،
قالدى ئۆ
كۆرستەلمەي سىرىمنى.
ئىزدىدىم كېپەك
مەن ئىستىگەن ئاشۇ تەگرىنى
قىلىشقا سەجدە.
يىرتتاي تېرەمنى
ئۆزۈم ئاڭا قالدى سىغالماي ،
كىسۋاللاي ئۆپۈقنى.
كۈتتىم كېپەك
سۆئاللىمغا سولاپ جاھاننى.
شەيئىللەرنى كۆزىتتەي ئەمدى
گۇمان كۆزىدە.
بۇ زاماننىڭ روبىنسونى مەن ،
قۇرۇپ چىقاي ئارىلىمنى
ئىككىنچى بىر دۇنيا يۈزىدە.

2

كەلدىم گۆركىرەپ...
سورىمىغىن كەلدىم قەيەردىن ؛
خالىغانچە ئاتىغىن مېنى:
بوران دەمسەن ،

Robinson

I must break out of
the echo's embrace
I will smash all the mirrors
which no longer reveal the slightest mystery
I must seek the god
whom I should pray to
I will skin myself
as my skin can no longer contain
my self in the horizon
I must leave
and address my questions to the world
I will watch everything
through doubtful eyes
I am the Robinson of the times
I will build my island
on the other side
of the world

2

I come drifting in
don't ask me from where
You can name me what you like:
a storm or the specter of death
I uproot your trees

ئەزرائىلنىڭ ئوبرازى ياكى.
باردىم قومۇرۇپ
ئىمزا قويغان دەرەخلىرىڭنى
كېلىشمىگە.
بارىمەن يالماپ
خەرىتەڭنى سىزغان سۇلارغا.
نۇرغۇنلىغان پۇتۇم ئاستىدا
يانچىلماقتا تارازىلىرىڭ.
ھېرىپ قالسام ،
ئۇلتۇرىمەن
جىجچەكلەردىن ياساپ تەختىمنى.
كېپىنەكلەر لەشكەرلىرىم.
قۇرماقتىمەن خانداننىلىقىمنى
گۈلدۈرماما ، شامااللاردىن...

3
بۇ دۇنيا
تۆرەلدى بىر تال قوۋۇرغامدىن.
بوغۇزۇمدا بىر ناخشا تېخىچە...
تەشۇششمنى يۇدۇپ كېلىمەن
بۇ يولدا -
ئەلمىساقتىن قىيامەتكىچە.

4
تەنھا ،
ئۇلتۇرىمەن يۇلىنىپ ئايفا.
مىنۇتلارنىڭ نەپەسلىرى
چىقىلماقتا تىنىقلىرىمدا.

40

that have sealed the agreement
I step forward, swallowing the map
you've drawn on the water
Your scales are crushed
beneath my feet
And when I'm tired
I sit on my throne of flowers
watching the butterflies
who are my soldiers
I build my kingdom
out of thunder and wind

3
This world
is created from my rib
There is still a song in my throat
as I carry the fears in my heart
along the road
from eternity to oblivion

4
Alone, I sit
leaning against the moon
The minutes breathe into me
paths fall before my feet
pleading for guidance
My mouth flows with lava
a stream runs through my veins

يوللار
ئايقىمغا يقىلىپ مېنىڭ ،
تىلەر ھىدايەت.
ئېغىزىمدا ماگمىلار ،
تومۇرۇمدا يۆگرەيدۇ باھار.

5
ھەر كۈنى سەھەر ،
ئۆۋسىدىن چىقىدۇ يوللار
ئوۋلاشقا مېنى.
مەخلۇقمەن يوچۇن ،
سۇئال ئۆنەر ماڭغان شۇنىمدىن.

6
خائىن تاغلار ،
قېنى مېنىڭ ئەكس سادايىم ؟!

5
Each morning
the roads leave their dens
to hunt me
I am a strange beast—
questions emerge from my footprints

6
Forbidden mountains
where is my echo?

الوصي على الذات

from

(1997)

مەن ئىزلەيمەن بالىلىقىمنى

مەن ئىزلەيمەن بالىلىقىمنى...
ئۆيىقۇدا ئىدىم
تاشلاپ قويۇپ مېنى يالغۇزلا ،
كەتتى يىراققا.
ئۆچوپ كەتتى ئەگىشىپ ئاتا
قۇچقاچلىرى جۇشۇمنىڭ.
تەبەسسۇمىم
توزۇپ كەتتى لەۋلىرىمدىن.

مەن ئىزدەيمەن بالىلىقىمنى...
سوردىم يوللاردىن ،
يۈرۈپ كەتتى يوللار چاقىرىپ ،
ئىزدەپ ئۇنى.
سوردىم شامالدىن ،
كەتتى شامال دەرىزە چىكىپ
ئىزدەپ ئۇنى.
سوردىم يامغۇردىن ،
كىرىپ كەتتى يامغۇر تۇپراققا ،
ئىزدەپ ئۇنى.
سوردىم ئايدىن ،
كەتتى ئايمۇ يىراق كۆككەرگە ،
ئىزدەپ ئۇنى.

مەن ئىزلەيمەن بالىلىقىمنى...
قايتتى يوللار ،
ئېلىپ كەلدى ئىزلىرىنى.
قايتتى شامال ،

46

I Am Looking for My Childhood

I am looking for my childhood. . .
I was asleep when it left me
and then vanished forever
The sparrows
in my dreams trailed behind
Ash covered my smiling lips

I am looking for my childhood. . .
I asked the path
and the path cried out
unknowingly
I asked the wind
and the wind rushed against the windows
unknowingly
I asked the rain
and the rain flowed into the ground
unknowingly
I asked the moon
and the moon drifted to the sky's edge
unknowingly

I am looking for my childhood. . .
The path returned
and brought me its footprints
The wind returned
and brought me its songs

ئۇلۇپ كەلدى ناخشلىرىنى.
قايتتى يامغۇر
ئۇلۇپ كەلدى كۆز ياشلىرىنى.
قايتتى ئاي ،
ئۇلۇپ كەلدى تىنىقلىرىنى.

مەن ئىزلەيمەن باللىقىمنى...
كەتىپتۇ ئۇ ئورماندىن ،
ئۇخلاپ ئۇندا بىر كىچە.
كەتىپتۇ ئۇ دېڭىزدىن ،
چۆمۈپ ئۇندا بىر قېتىم.
كەتىپتۇ ئۇ بۇلۇتتىن ،
تاراپ ئۇندا چىچىنى.
كەتىپتۇ ئۇ ئۇيۇقتىن ،
ئارقىسسفا بىر قاراپ.

مەن ئىزدەيمەن باللىقىمنى...
باھاردىكى گۈلىمدۇ دەيمەن ،
يازدىكى باشاقىمدۇ دەيمەن ،
كۈزدىكى غازاڭىمدۇ دەيمەن ،
قىشتىكى قارىمدۇ دەيمەن ،
ئوتىمدۇ دەيمەن ،
سۈمدۇ دەيمەن ،
مەن ئىزلەيمەن باللىقىمنى...

The rain returned
and brought me its tears
The moon returned
and brought me its breath

I am looking for my childhood...
The forest said it left me
after I fell asleep in her branches
The sea said it left me
after I bathed in her waters
The cloud said it left me
after a flash of remembering
The horizon said it left me
after I glanced behind me

I am looking for my childhood...
Is it a flower in spring?
Is it a spike of wheat in summer?
Is it a yellow leaf in autumn?
Is it snow in winter?
Is it fire?
Is it water?
I am looking for my childhood...

سلام العاشق

رأسها عند ساعدي صياح الطيور عبر الزجاج.
نومٌ
كأنه الصبح ،
كأنه شمسٌ تشرق من فوران الدم.
أيل يجري في العروق
يفرش درباً لا ينتهي
يمتد من الجبين
حيث تتنفس بانسجام طاغٍ.

قلبها قريب من قلبي ،
وتنعكس أهدابها في عينيّ:
ألمح سرباً من حمائم أو جثث الجنود...
أرى انفجار الزمن الداني من هالة النهدين.
يا ابنة الإيقاع ،
يا ذات الأب القاسي ،
يا شهوة تقفز من عيوني
كالفهد
كشمسٍ تتمرغ بطحالب البحر.

سلاماً أيها السرير يا جسداً بعدد المرايا:
مرآة جريمةٍ تنأى في الألق ،
مرآة ضحكةٍ خاطفة كالبشب ،
ودم يتفجر من الصخور في المرآة.
طوبى سلام المرايا ،
طوبى لسلام الليل في سحُر العتبات.

رأسها عند ساعدي — في كل ينبوع فيها احتدامي ،

The Peace of the Lover

Her head on my arm
The screeching of birds outside the window
Sleep. . .
Morning
sun shines upon boiling blood
A deer runs in the veins
makes an unending path
that extends from her forehead
to her breath
a soft, pure harmony

Her heart nears mine
Her eyelashes reflect in my eyes
I see a flock of doves, the corpses of soldiers. . .
I see explosions of time approaching her hallowed breasts
O daughter of rhythm
of the unjust father
O lust that leaps from my eyes
like a leopard
like a sun that plunges into seagrass

Peace to you O bed
mirror of the body's multiplicity
mirror of a transgression that fades in the spark
mirror of the quickening jasper laugh
as blood breaks free from the mirrored rocks
Blessed is the peace of mirrors
Blessed is the peace of night at the threshold

ونوم يشمل فجر الرماد كأنها أوشكت عليّ من كل صوب.

لَكَم خفيفة يدها المشعة ،

تلك الحيوان الصغير

الذي يغفو بعذوبة على صدري.

وعلى ثغرها العالي الدوران ،

المرفرفِ الآن في حقول الحلم

ظلُّ ابتسامة ،

فجرُ ابتسامة ،

يذكرني بهناء الطير في عش الصنوبر ،

في ساعة قصية من الليل

ساعةً تُقبل الريح المخصبة

ورأسها عند ساعدي مواعيد النبات.

Her head on my arm is the source of my being within her
Sleep brings dawn's ash
as if she closes in from every direction
How light is her hand that glows
on my chest
as if a small animal resting sweetly
And there, across her mouth
in a dreaming field
flies the shadow of her smile
the birth of her smile, memory
of a bird in a pine nest
In the late hour of the night
the hour of the sowing wind
her head on my arm, the season of harvest

كأنْ

from

As Though

(1998)

ئەجەپ ئۇغۇر غەم باستى مېنى

"ئەجەپ ئۇغۇر غەم باستى مېنى"
دەيدۇ كېچە ،
"ئۆلۈۋاتقان يۇلتۇزلار باستى..."

"ئەجەپ ئۇغۇر غەم باستى مېنى"
دەيدۇ ئۇششۇك ،
"تۆل قىبلۇۋاتقان كەچلەر باستى..."

"ئەجەپ ئۇغۇر غەم باستى مېنى"
دەيدۇ بوسۇق ،
"يىپىق قالغان ئىششىكلەر باستى..."

"ئەجەپ ئۇغۇر غەم باستى مېنى"
دەيدۇ يۈرەك ،
"بوسۇقلار باستى..."

ئاتقاندا تاڭ ، دەر زېمىن چوقۇم:
ئاھ...‟
ئەجەپ ئۇغۇر نۇر باستى مېنى ،
يۇلتۇزلار باستى كەچلەر باستى ،
ئىششىكلەر باستى بوسۇقلار باستى
يۈرەكلەر باستى!»

How Weary I Am

"How weary I am,"
says the night,
"of dying stars..."

"How weary I am,"
says the door,
"of widowed nights..."

"How weary I am,"
says the threshold,
"of shut doors..."

"How weary I am,"
says the heart,
"of abandoned thresholds..."

And as dawn breaks it says,
"Oh... how weary I am
of stars and nights,
of doors, thresholds
and hearts!"

الأسلاف

\

رياحاً بهبوب الأنجم الباردة
تعبرون جفنيّ الآن ،
يا مقيمين في قارة الموت —
هنا: في جسدي ،
يا أسلافي...
لكم كان حزنكم شاحباً كالكتب ،
وجوهكم هادئة كالشموع
المغبرة
في المعبد المهجور.
وأنا
على شاطئكم الرملي أغفو
كمركبكم القديم.

٢

أسلافي...
يا من سيحيون من بعدي ،
ومحمولين على إعصار من مسافات حالكة
يا من استفرقوا عمراً مديداً من الشرود
قبل أن يبلغوا سن الرشد
وتبلغهم طير المشيئة الجارحات...

يا ثماراً كفت ، في الأوان ، عن البصر
ولم ترتم عن غصون الليل
الخضراء...

Predecessors

1
As the wind blows off cold stars
you pass beneath my eyelids
O residents of death's continent
here, in my body
O predecessors

Your sorrow is as pale as the words
in a book, your faces as quiet
as the dust-covered candles
in a deserted temple
And upon your sandy shore
I sleep: your ancient boat

2
My predecessors. . .

You who will live on after me
took a long leave of absence
carried away by a hurricane into dark distances
before ripening
before the raptors descended

O fruits of lost days
suspended on the green branches of night
Time weaved its shining web

يا من نسج الزمن السحيق خيوطه المضيئة
على وجوههم
يا من انتصبوا باباً خفياً، نائياً في الأبد
وأقدامهم عتبة نازفة...

وصلني بريدكم دون عنوان المرسل إليه
فأرسلت في أثركم غيهب الظلمات.

across your faces
You who stand like invisible doors against the eternal past
your feet bleeding thresholds

Your letters I receive bear no return address
so I send out the darkness to search for you

عزلة

يا بحر...
لا جفنٌ لك يغمض... كيف لي أنام!
هذا الشاطئ المهجور — قلبي
موحش غير أن موجك الشريد
يرفرف على الصخور ،
يحدق بي طويلاً...
يعود يتوارى
في الظلام.

Solitude

O sea. . .
you don't close your eyes
so how can I sleep!
And this abandoned shore, my heart
is desolate
Your running waves wash over the rocks
and gaze out at me for so long
before returning to the darkness
you vanish

باشقا بىر ئايىنىڭ كۆتشىشىدە ئولتۇراقلىشىش

قۇش ، دەيرىزە ۋە تولۇنئاي ئوتتۇرىسسدىكى يوچۇن مۇناسۋۆت توغرىسسدا

كىرپىك قاققىچە
دەيرىزەمدىن ئوتتۇپ كەتتى قۇش ،
تولۇن ئاينى ئوتتۇردىن يىرسپ ئىككىگە...

يۈز بەرگەن ئۇ شۇڭداق بىر قىپتىم ،
بالا ئىدىم ئۇچاغ ۋەتەندە.

مالايىلار

باققىنىمدا تۈنجى رەت كۆككە ،
توۋلدىم: دادا...!
يۇرەر ئىدى ئۇ
يەلكىسىدە يۆدۈپ قۇياشنى.

باققىنىمدا تۈنجى رەت كۆككە ،
توۋلدىم: ئانا...!
يۇرەر ئىدى ئۇ
باش ئۈستىدە كۆتۈرۈپ ئاينى.

ھەسرەت

ھىچكىم
ھەبىت سوغسى كۆتۈرۈپ كەلمەيدۇ يولدا...
يالغۇزلا شۇ كونا تولۇن ئاي
يىراقتىكى كەپىسسدىن سىلار مەڭزىمنى.

Dwelling in the Warmth of Other Moons

Of the strange relationship between a bird, a window, and the moon

In a glance
the bird passed before my window
and divided the moon in half. . .
This happened once
when I was a child in my homeland

Diligence

For the first time, I looked at the day
and called out, "Father. . . !"
The sun was a bundle of firewood
on his shoulder

For the first time, I looked at the night
and called out, "Mother. . . !"
The moon was a water jar
on her head

Grief

No one
comes here bearing gifts
Only the old moon
from its remote hut
touches my cheek

ئۇمىد

ئۇمىد

شۇ قىزىققاق ئاي...
قوللىرىمدىن يىتىلەپ
ئاپرار مېنى ھايات ئالدىغا
ئەپۇ سورا دەپ.
تاشلاپ قويۇپ ئىككىمىزنى
سۆيۈشكەنچە ،
دەرەخ كەينىدىن
قىزىقچىدەك مارىلار ئۇمىد.

يالغۇزلۇق

دېرىزەمگە يىقىنلاپ گۈگۈم
يىغلايدۇ ئۆكسۈپ...
كەردۇ ئاي
قىيا ئۈچىپ ئىشىكىمنى
قۇلاق سالار تاك ئاتقىچە
شېپىرلىرىدىغا.
ئۈنتۈپ كۆلداندا موخۇركسسنى
جىقىپ كېتەر
ھارغىن ،
ئۇيقۇلۇق.

Hope

Hope
is a curious moon. . .
It pulls me by my hand
and guides me toward life
for me to say I'm sorry
It leaves us in the park
and as we kiss
hope hides as if it's a clown, smiling,
behind a tree

Loneliness

Once when dusk
fell across my window
I was weeping
and the moon entered
opening the door quietly
and stayed with me till morning
listening to my poems
When the moon left
me exhausted, dazed
it forgot its burning cigarette in the ashtray

ئانا

بىر كۈن
ئۈزدەپ كەلسە سېنى پەرىشتە ،
كۈپتەرسەنمۇ ئۈمىتكىلى
بالىلرنى جەننەتنىك ؟
يىغلارمىكىن ئاي پەرىزات
ئۆتتۇەپلىپ قۇياش كەينگە ،
رومال قىلسام دەپ
كىپىنىڭنى...
ئانا ،
كۈتتىرەلمەس قەبرەڭنى تۇپراق!

ئەسلىمىلەر

يادىڭدىمۇ ؟
دېدى ئاي ،
ئۆخلاپ قالغان چاغدا ئەركىنلىك
كوچىدىلا غەرق مەست
ئەيقاجقانتى ئۆنى يۈلتۇزلار ؛
شۇ كۈندىن باشلاپ
پەيدا بولغان ئىسدىك سەن ، قۇياش!

يادىڭدىمۇ ؟
دېدى قۇياش ،
ھۆجرامغا مەست ئۆسۈپ كىرگىنىك ؟
شۇ كۈندىن باشلاپ
قۇغلۇۋەتكەن سېنى قەبىلەم
يىراق كىچمگە.

68

Mama

Mama,
the day the angel
comes looking for you
will you go with him
to nurse the babies in heaven?
And the shroud. . .
will you give it to the moon nymph
as a sacred garment for her head?
And your tomb. . .
the earth isn't strong enough to hold it

Memories

The moon said,
"Do you remember
when freedom fell asleep drunk in an alley
and was then abducted by the stars?
Since that day
you, sun, have appeared in public!"

The sun replied,
"Do you remember
when you crashed into my room
drunk?
Since that day
my tribe has banished you, moon,
beyond the night!"

ئايدىڭ چۈش

كىرگەندە سەھەر ،
كارۋېتىمغا يىقىنلاشقاندا
ياستۇقۇمنىڭ ئۈستىدە كۆردۈم
بىر ئايدىڭ چۈشنى.
ناخشا ئېيتار ئىدى دەرىزە ،
شامال چالار دەرەخ غولىنى.

سېغىنىش

ھېلىغىچە
تارىم چۆلىدە
داپ ئۈسسۈلى ئويىنامدۇ شامال ؟
ئولتۇرامدۇ تولۇن ئاي
بوغدا كۆلىدە
چاچلىرىنى ئۆرۈپ قىرىق تال ؟

ئانام غېمىنىڭ قالدۇق كۆزۈكى

يولتۆزلار —
ناخشىلىرى ئانامنىڭ
بۇشۇۋكۈمدە ئەلەيلەتكەن.

ئاي —
چۈشۈمدۇر مېنىڭ
ئاسمان ئەينكىدە ئەكس ئەتكەن.

كېچە —
ئانام غېمىنىڭ قالدۇق كۆزۈكى.

Moonlit Dream

Morning
approached my bed
I saw the moonlit dream on my pillow
The windows were singing
and the wind played the strings
of the tree trunks

Nostalgia

To this day
in the Tarim Desert
does the wind still dance the tambourine dance?
And the moons. . .
are they still in Boghda Lake
weaving their hair into forty braids?

Remnants of Grief

The stars told me
that they were nothing but my mother's hums
at my cradle

The moon told me
that it was nothing but a dream of mine
reflected in the sky's mirror

The night told me
that it was nothing but the burning remnants
of my mother's grief

يالتىراش

قاچاندىن بۇيان بۇ يالتىراش كۆزلىرىڭدىكى ؟
قالغىننىدا بولۇپ سەۋدايى چىڭگىمجۇشنىڭ قۇياشى ؟
ئۈمىدسىزلىك ئەۋجىگە ياكى چىققىننىدا تولۇن ئاي ؟
ياكى بولمىسا
ئۆلۈمىگىنىڭ تىبرەن سايىسى چۈشكىنىندە تاشلارغا ؟

باھار

باھار
شۇ كەپىسىز بالا ،
ئويغىتىدۇ زېمىننى
چىغ تىقىپ قۇلقىغا.
پاراقلاپ كۆلۈپ ،
سۇ چاچىدۇ يۈزىڭگە
ئۇسسىم رەستلىرىدە ئۇگدەپ قالغان خاتىرىلەرنىڭ.
بىچارە...
ئازاپلىنار قانجىلىك
بىلسە ئەگەر بىر يىتىم ئاي ئىككەنلىكىنى ؟!

ئازاب يولى

قوۋۇۋۇرغامدىن ياراتتىم مەن قانجىلاپ
سېنى ، شېئىر ، كەچۈرگەيسەن گۇناھلىرىمنى.
يۈرمە كەتمەن...
يۈرمە كەتمەن ئازاب يولىدا
كۆتۈرگەنچە مۇرەمدە ئايلىرىڭنى.

Shine

What causes that shine in your eyes?
The sun's madness at noon
or the moon in despair?
Or perhaps the deep shadow of your death
cast across the stone?

Spring

It is spring. . .
A naughty boy
inserts a straw into the ear of the earth
disturbing its deep sleep
He laughs and laughs,
drips water into the thoughts
that have fallen asleep on the sidewalk of my memory
Poor boy. . .
how great his suffering when he realizes
he is an orphan moon

Via Dolorosa

How many times have I created you from my rib
poem, forgive me
my sins
Heavy with your many moons
I walk the Via Dolorosa

ئۈرۈمچى

......

كۆلەڭگىلەر كېتتىدۇ ، كېپلىدۇ...

يۇرەر غازاگلار رەستلەردىن رەستلەرگە...

ئىشىك قىقىپ يۇردۇ شامال ئەگەشتۈرۈپ پەسللەرنى...

توختايدۇ ئاي

ئوربۇپلىپ موخۈركسسنى يۇرۇپ كېتتىدۇ...

ئۆزۈك-ئۆزۈك پويىز ئاۋازى ياشلار بىلەن نەملەنگەن...

......

بۆركۆتسىز ئۇۋا

ئۈرۈمچى...

جەگچى

ئاي نۇرىدا بىر جۆپ قورام تاش

لەۋلەربىمدۇ

ياربىلانغان جەگچى كەبى ياتقان بۇ تاغنىك ؟

ئارسسىدىن بۆلدۆقلايدۇ تىمتاس بىر بۆلاق

قانىمدۇ ئۇ ؟

ياكى سۆز-كالام ؟

74

Urumqi

. . . .

Shades come and go. . .

Wind begs on the streets with the seasons. . .

The moon pauses

lights a rolled cigarette

and continues on. . .

Train whistle wet with tears. . .

. . . .

Eagle's nest empty. . .

Urumqi. . .

Warrior

The two rocks beneath the moonlight:

Are they the lips of the warrior

who was felled on the mountain?

And the spring flowing silently between them:

Is it blood?

Or speech?

الطيف

يلوذ الرمل بصمته ،
والبحر مقفلة أجراسه ، المراكب في قلبي
يهدهدها النعاس.
وقريباً من موجة هدأت
يلمع حزن مع الصدف ،
كان لا بد أن يكون مشرقاً ،
فها أنت قدمت ، أيها الطيف...
غالباً تجيئني على الشاطئ في المساء ،
ملاكاً
ذا وجه حنون ومرعب
مسائلاً عينيّ عن المكان الذي فيه
سأموت...

Shadow

Sand shelters its silence
The sea has locked its bells
Sleep rocks the boat in my heart
A wave calms close by
sadness shines with shells
with brightness
you come, O shadow. . .
You often appear on the shore in the evening
as an angel
with an affectionate and terrifying face
gaze into my eyes in wonder
of the place where I will die

مسار

في السكون
سكون الليل
الليل الذي يوشك على النور
النور الذي كانه الزمن على جفنيكِ للتو
في النور الذي يغدو المسار
كان جفناك منفتحينِ على النور
منغلقينِ على المسار
المسار الذي تنامين الآن فيه
كما أتكلم بلا سبب
دون انقطاع.

Track

In stillness, the stillness
of night, the night
that is about to light up
the light that is time on your closed eyes
becomes the track in the light
Your eyes open to the light
close on the track
the track you now sleep on
as I speak without cause
uninterrupted

ئۇيغۇر دىيارى، ئەك يىراق سۆرگۈنگاھ!

...مەن قانچە رەت پاناھلاندىم ئۆزۈمدە
بىشىمفا بۇ بالدۇر كەلگەن تەنھالىقتا...
ھەمدە كۆزۈم، بەزى چاغلاردا،
ھەسرەتلىرىم جىمىققان ھامان
يۇمۇلار تېزلا،
ھىچ قالدۇرماي ماڭا «مەن تەنھا»
دەيدىغان پۇرسەت.

ئىسمىنىڭ زېمىنىندىكى
شۇ قەدەمىمى ئۆزىنىڭ بۇلۇك-يۇشقىمقىدا
ئۆچۈپ قالغان جىنچىراق توغرىسىدا
بىر دەملىك خىيالدىن كېيىن،
ئۇيغاتماقتا مېنى يۇچۇن بىر تۆيۈفۇ:
زاۋال تاپقان كىتابپارنىڭ قۇرلىرى ئارا
سەرسانلىق پەرىشتىسى سىپىرىدە
«ئۇيغۇر دىيارى، ئەك يىراق سۆرگۈنگاھ!»
دەپ
ئىبغىز ئاچقان قۇشلارنى ئىزدەش
پەيتى ئەمدى كەلدى، دېگەندەك.

ئىستەيمەن بۇدەم
ئۇنۇتۇسام دەپ قۇشلار قىلفان سۆزلەرنى،
تاپسام دەيمەن
قەدەملىرىم قانىفان شۇ تون زېمىننى.
قانداقسىگە ئۇيىلماي
ئۆزاقتىن بۇيان ئاگلىفانلار ھەققىدە؟!
چۈنكى ئاۋاز بۇرار مەندە يۇنۇۇلۇشنى،

80

Uyghurland, the Farthest Exile

In my early isolation, I'd often withdraw
homeward into my heart. Then, as my grief
subsided, my eyes would quickly close
not giving me a chance
to say, "I am alone. . ."

After days of staring
at lit candles (the flame
no longer burns in the corner
of the old house in the land of memory)
a strange feeling woke me up
to the time of searching
for the birds
who pronounced the words of the Wandering Angel
between lines of buried books,
"Uyghurland,
the farthest exile!"

Now I wish to forget
what emerged from the tongues of birds
and accept a land of darkness
where my feet bleed. To stop
thinking of the ancient things I've heard
for the voices have shifted direction in me
so that am I indeed what the birds pronounced?

مەن كۆرۈندۈم شۇگۇا ئۆزۈمگە:
گوياكى مەن قۇشلار قلغان ئاشۇ شۆزلەر .

بۇ يەردە ،
شۇگغۇماقتا مۇجمەل ئاي
كۆزلرىمنى باسقان كەجكى شەيەقتە ،
تەجەللىيەت بۇلمقدا باغاشلىغاندەك
سەرسان ئويۇمنى .
«قەدەم تاشلا مەن تامان ، »
خىتاپ قلار ماگا جنجىراق ،
«زاۋال تايقان زىمنىمدىن چىق ئەمدى ،
شۇنجە يارقىن ئاۋاز بىلەن ئۇغىز ئاچقىن
ئەركىن ھالدا:
ئۇيغۇر دياري! - دەپ» .

سۆز ھالىتى ئىجرە مەن
كەلتۈرمەكتە ئىدىم كونا قۇياشىمنى ئەسلىگە ،
بار ئىدى ھەم بەلكى زاماننىك
كۆندۈزدنىمۇ باشقا نەقىل كەلتۈرشى ،
ئايان بولدى ، شۇگگلاشقا ،
جۇشەنگلى بولمايدىغان ، سەۋەپسىز بىر بۆرۈدەك ،
ھەمدە بىر خىل گۆزگالىق كەبى ،
بىز بۇ يەرگە كەلگەندىن بۇيان .

مەن سورايمەن ئۆزۈمدىن شۇ لەھزە ھەققىدە:
قانداق زىمىن بولۇشى مۇمكىن ؟!
قۇلاق سالىمەن: ئۇندا ئازاپ چاقىرماقتا ،
شۇنجە يىراق بىر جايدا ،
ئۇيغەمتەدۇ مەندە ھەتتا مۇساپىنىك ئىشتىياقنى ،
قەبرىلەردە قاغجىرىغان شاخلارغا قونغان

82

Here, the mysterious moon
falls, heavy twilight on my shut eyes
as if embracing a stray thought
in the springtime of reincarnation
"Come toward me," the candle beckons,
"you must leave this extinguished land
to shout freely with a vital voice,
'Uyghurland!'"

From within the folds of speech
I recovered the ancient sun
Perhaps time
was measure without day
as it leapt toward us like a wolf
for no reason
impossible to comprehend
from the moment we arrived here
the moment I questioned myself,
"What land could that be?"
I listen to the cries of suffering there
faraway, waking inside me a nostalgic distance
like the caws of crows
on bare branches in a cemetery
Thus the widening sea
of exile within me
where the guardian birds
signal the next island

قاغا ئۇنىدەك...
ئويلاندۇرۇپ مېنى دېگىز كەگلىكىنى ،
سۈرگۈنگاھنىڭ مابەينىدە .
ئۇندا يەنە ماڭا ھامى شۇ قۇشلار
كەلگۈسى ئاراللاردىن بېرەر بىشارەت .

بەلكى قېتىپ قېلىشى شامااللارنىڭ
ئەتراپىمگلاردا ،
ئەي ، ئۇزاقلاپ كەتكۈچىلەر ،
تەقدىردۇر تېرەن ئۆلۈمنىڭ كارسىزلىقىغا -
ئائىت بولغان ئېتىقادنىڭ تۇپەيلىدىن ،
ھەمدە مەن ئۆزگە شەيئى ئەمەس ،
پەقەت
ئۆزۈملا بولۇپ كەلگەن سەۋەبىدىن.
شۇنداقتىمۇ ،
بۇيۇك قۇشلار پەرۋاز ئەيلىگەن
سامااللاردىن قەتئىينەزەر ،
مەن يەنە تونۇش كۈينىڭ قاناتلىرى ئاستىدا
ئويغانغان دەمدە ،
تەلتۆكۈس سۈكۈتۈمدە مەن تۇرغان زېمىن
ئىزتىراپقا چۆشكەن دەمدە ،
كۆرمە كىتمەن
پۈتكۈل شەيئىلەر
ئايلانماقتا ئەتراپىمدا زۇلمەتتە...

ئىزلىەيدۇ تەن ، شۇندىاقلا ،
كۆك تۇماندا تېپىسقىلاپ يۈرۈپ ئەرۋاھتەك ،
خۇلاسلاش ئۈچۈن ئازاپ شەكىلدىن
ئاشكارىلانغان شەيئىلەرنىڭ يۈنۈلۈشىنى ،

84

Perhaps the immobile winds around you
O distant outliers
were a fated certainty, a futility
in the depths of death and of being
purely one's self,
one's pure self
Whatever space the great birds fly through
I wake beneath the wings
of the famous ode
the place I am in, in
silence, disturbed
I watch
everything revolve around me
in darkness. . .

The body searches
circles like a ghost in blue fog
to discern the direction of what was foretold
as suffering
and form a dream
it can reside in
and name

Later in sorrow, the birds
would often withdraw
homeward into my heart. Their eyes,
as my thoughts
subsided, would quickly close
not giving me a chance to say,

ھەم قايتىدىن تۆزەپ چىقىش ئۈچۈن چۈشنى ،
ئىستەپ ئۆندا ئولتۇراقلىشىپ قېلىشنى ،
ئاگا ئىسىم ئاتا قىلىشنى...

قۇشلار شۆنجە پاناھلاندى قەلبىمدە
ۋۇجۇدۇمنى سۆر باسقان يىراق زاۋالدا...
ھەم كۆزلىرى ، بەزى چاغلاردا ،
خىياللىرىم جىمىقىقان ھامان ،
يۈمۈلار تېزلا
ھېچ قالدۇرماي ئاگا ئويى-خىياللىرىنى
دەيدىغان پۈرسەت:
«گۈزەل ئىدى كۈندۈز تولمۇ
نېمىدىغەن قاباھەت-ھە ، بۇ!
چىقىلماقتا قەدەملىرىڭ كۆلدۈرمىسلىرى
پاسىللىرىدا يۈرتلارنىڭ ،
ھەمدە ئايال ئەمچەكلىرى شورلىشۇاتقان -
رۆجەكتىكى قۇياشىنىڭ ئەكس ساداسى
ئەترايىڭدا ئۆزلىكسىز ياگرىماقتا:
ئۇيغۇر دىيارى ،
يىراق سۈرگۈنگاھ!...»

"That day
was the most beautiful day."
O the terror—
as the bells of your footsteps break
at the border of each country,
and the echo
of sun shines through a window
onto a woman's rusted bosom—
that repeats around you without disruption,
"Uyghurland,
the farthest exile!"

في أطلال سومر حيث أقيم

from

IN RUINS OF SUMER
WHERE I RESIDE

(2003)

قۇم كارۋاتتكى ئاخشام

بۇ يەردە ، قۇم كارۋۇتتمزدا ، ئاي ئۇيقۇسدىن ئويغىنىپ
ھاكلاشقان دېگىنزنى ئۆز ئورنىدىن يۆتكەۋاتىدۇ
سۆيۈملۈكۈم ، مانا بۇ - خىيالىڭنىڭ تېشى
دولقۇنلاۋاتىدۇ
تەندە سارغىمىشقا باشلىغان باشاقلار ئىجرە
نۇر بولۇپ ئبقۋاتىدۇ

قاغىلارنىڭ ئۈنىدىكى قاراڭغۇ ئىككى قولۇم
قۇمدا بۇؤغۇننى چوشەۋاتقان ئىككى قىبىق ئىدى
ئۈندا
پەرىشان سۆيگۈنمنىڭ كېچمىز تېنەپ قالغان ئۇپۆكى
لەۋلىرمنىڭ ئوڭگۇل-دوڭگۇلدا ئۆلۈپ قالغان جەرەندۇر

شەپەق ، تېخجە ، يايراقلسرى تۆكۈلمۈاتقان پاچاقلسرم
چىبلۇاتقان بىر كۈي
گويا قىنىمدىن كەپتەر ئۆچقاندەك
يىلتىزلاردا مىۇللەرنىڭ ھەيرانلىقىنى قوزغايدۇ

سۆيۈملۈكۈم ، سىپەنىش پالچىسىنى ئاگلىدىڭمۇ ؟
يارىللانغان ئەتىرگۈلۈمدىن بوشلۇق ئۆرلىگەندە
سۇلرىڭدا سەرسان بولغان بىر زېمىننى چوشىدىم
شامالدەك سوقۇپلا كارۋاتتنىڭ قۇملىرىدا توزىغان ئىڭراشنى
تىلىمنىڭ ئاستىدا يەنە بىر رەت كۆشەۋاتاتنم

بۇلاقلارنىڭ سايسى چوشكەن يۈرىكىم
تىكەنلەرگە يىقىلغان تورغايغا ئايلاندى
بىلكىككنىڭ بەرگىدە شەبنەم بولۇپ قۇرۇپىمەن
كۆزگۆم چوشكەن ئاغزىڭدا يۇلتۇز بولۇپ يانمەن

90

Evening on a Bed of Sand

Here on our bed of sand
a moon wakes from its slumber
and lifts the frozen sea from its place
Here is the stone of your absence, my lover,
that undulates, flows
as light through ears of wheat
yellowing in the body
My darkening hands among the cries of ravens
are two boats in the sand
as the dream turns to foam
the evening kiss of my sad lover
feels like a dead gazelle against my rough lips

The twilight is a melody
My legs move through fallen leaves
awakening the wonder of fruit within the roots
—a pigeon takes flight from my blood
Did you, my love, hear the oracle's reminiscence?
As the sky evaporates from your wounded rose
I dream of an island in your waters
from beneath my tongue a gasp
escapes and fades onto the bed of sand

My heart shadowed by the water's source
turns into a skylark that alights on the thorns
I dry like dew on the corollas of your forearms
I glow like a star in your twilight mouth

سۆيۈملۈكۈم ، خالىفىنىڭنى سۆزله:
بىر ئاي دىگمزنى يۈتكەۋاتامتى ؟
ياكى ئۆ ، ئاخشامنىڭ قۇملىرىدىكى كارۋۇتمزمۇ ؟
نۇر بولۇپ باشاقلاردا تاش ئاقتىمۇ ؟
ياكى پات ئارىدا يۈز بەردىگان بىر غايىبلىق ؟

قۇلقمغا يىراقتىن ئاڭلىنىۋاتقنى
سىنىڭ قەددەمىلرىڭ ئىككەنلىكىنى يەنە بىر رەت جەزملەشتۈرىمەن
ھەتتا زېمىنمۇ ، سۆيۈملۈكۈم ، پاچاقلىرىم شادلانغان ئاشۇ يەردە
ماگا ئوخشاش
شەھۇەتلەرگە ئاز قالغان كېپلىندەك
تىترەۋاتىمىۋ

ئانىدىن قەلبىمدە شەپەق ئويغاندى
ئۈنىڭ يۈكسەك سايىسى بالكونلارنىڭ ئاخشىمىغا چىچىلغان
كارۋۇتىنىڭ قۇملىرىدا قوڭغۇراقلار جىرىڭكلاپ -
سەدەپلەرنىڭ
ئۆز دولقۇنلىرىنىڭ شاۋقۇنىدىكى بۇ تېنىمنىڭ سەدەپلىرىنىڭ ئۈسىدە
شاراب كەشنەۋاتىمىۋ
ئاي قالدۇق شارابمىز
ئاسمان بولسا ھەسەن-ھۈسەن چاقنىغان رومكىمىز شىدى
بەئەينى مەن ، سۆيۈملۈكۈم ، بىر ئورما مۇراسمىدا ئۇزۇپ يۈرگەندەك !
سەنمۇ مەنىدەك ، بىرەر قېتىم ، سەرخۇشلۇقتىنىڭ ھوزۇرىنى سۆرگەنمىدىك
ئاشىق ، بەئەينى ، يولتۈزۈلارنى يىغلىغاندەك !
ھەمدە غايىبلىق ئۈز تېنىنى مەندە داۋاملاشتۈردى

مانا بۇ بىزنىڭ كارۋۇتمز ، سۆيۈملۈكۈم
ئۆ ، كىرپىكلىرىمز ئارىسىدىكى تار بىر بوشلۇقتا تەۋرىنەتتى
بارماقلىرىم ئارىسدا دولقۇنلار ئۇرىلىشۇاتامتى
ياكى قوللىرىمز بىر-بىرىگە كىرىشۇاتامتى ؟!

92

Speak, lover, of what you desire
Was it the moon that stole the sea?
And the evening on a bed of sand?
Did the stone flow as light through the ears of wheat?
Or was it only imminent absence?

Once more I can make out the distant
sound of your footsteps
Even the earth, my love, trembles as I do
like a bride at the edge of desire's delight

Twilight falls in my heart
Shadows stretch across the balconies
Bells ring above the bed of sand
Wine swirls in a memory of shells
echo of the tide's roar
The moon is at the wine's lees
the sky iridescent glass
I am lost, my love, in a festival of wheat
Were you once as ecstatic as I, crying to the stars,
while the absence continued to grow within me?
It is our bed, my love,
drifting in the narrow space beneath our eyes
waves splashing between my fingers
our hands intertwined

The evening on a bed of sand is salt
on a wound, it is plunging alone
into the depths

بىر تۆزلۈق جاراھەتتۆر بىزنىڭ ئاخشامدىكى قۇم كارۋېتىمىز
گويا ئو ، ئۆزى يالغۇز ، سايىلەرگە چۆكمۈاتىدۇ

ئۇلۇغ-كىچىك تىنىپ پىچىرلايمەن:
ئەي ، سەرسان... ئەي ، قۇشلار چۇقانى...
ئەي ، قېنىمنىڭ ئەينىكى يىتتۈرگەن چەھەر...
ئەي ، كېبمەم... ئەي ، قىرغاقلىرىم بىلەن بىللە تېنەپ يۈرگۈچى...
ئەي ، تېنىمنىڭ زۇلمەتتە كۆيگەن شام...
ئەي ، قىزىلقىمدىكى ئاتەش...
ئەي ، ھاكلىرىمفا يېفىپ كەتكەن دېڭىز قۇشلىرى...
ئەي ، كارۋېتىمدا سوزۇلۇپ ياتقان تەنھالىق...
ئەي ، ئەمچىكىمنىڭ ئارىسىفا ئۆۋا سالغان قۇش... ئەي ، قاقاس يەر...
ئەي ، دېڭىز... ئەي ، قىرغاقلىرى پۈتۈن دۇنيا ئاياللىرى...

سەنمۇ مەندەك ئۇلۇغ-كىچىك تىنىپ پىچىرلامسەن:
ئەي ، كۆيىۈك بىفىم
ئەي ، تىكەنلەر ئۈستىدىكى تورغاي
ئەي ، مېنىڭ چىچچەك يىشى دەپ تەسەۋۋۇر قىلغىنىم
تەن ئاخشىمدا مەن سېنىڭ شەمۇۋتىنگۈنىڭ ياۋا بۇقىسى ئىدىم
مېنىڭ قەبرىلىرىم ئاشۇ كارۋۈاتلار شاۋقۇنلىغان يەردە
ئۇندا! ئۇلۇۆكلەر كارۋۇنى چىدىرلىرىنى شەپەققە تىكمىدۇ
ھەمدە
ئاخشامنىڭ ساھىللىرىدا
قۇملىرى قۇرۇپ
ھاكلىشىپ كەتكەن يالىڭگاچ تەنلەرگە
تىمتاسلىق قانات يايدۇ

94

I sigh, whispering:
O displacement. . . O clamor of birds. . .
O face that my bloodied mirror scatters. . .
O my boat... O you who strayed onto my shores. . .
O candle that brightens the darkness of my body. . .
O fire of my virginity. . .
O flock of gulls in my dreams. . .
O dreariness that lies in my bed. . .
O bird nesting in my arms. . . O wilderness. . .
O sea. . . and the shore of the lovers. . .

Do you sigh
Do you whisper
O my dark garden
O skylark on the thorns
I imagine you as the tears of a flower. . .
I was the wild bull of your lust
in the evening of the body
My grave is there in the roar of the bed
where the dead pitch their tents in the twilight
and stillness spreads its wings onto the naked bodies
on which the sand crystallizes
into the shores of evening

كمن يسير في حلمه

١

حين أبكي كنتِ تُقبلين لإرضاعي
حين أبكي كنتِ تهمّين بهدهدتي
ضامةً كليتي إلى حضنك الدافئ
حين أبكي كنت تطعميني قطعة سكّر
كانت في فمك
كنت تعرفين أبجدية بكائي
والآن ، يا أماه
حين أبكي
تتدحرج الدنيا على خدك
ولا تعرفين ماذا تفعلين !

٢

إلى الآن
كأجراس القافلة
ترن قريباً من مسامعي
هدهدتك الحزينة يا أماه
إلى الآن
ما زال تحت لساني العاق
طعم مخاضك المر
جئتُ إلى الدنيا
حاملاً على كتفيّ أمانيك
كأنك وهبتي الإحساس نفسه
وأنا في المهد
لذا ، ربما ، قستُ أسناني على حلمة ثدييك

As One Who Walks in a Dream

1
When I cried, you gave me your breast
When I cried, you gathered me
into your warm arms
When I cried, you fed me a morsel of sugar
from your own mouth
You knew the alphabet of my cry
Now, Mama, when I cry
the world rolls down your cheeks
and you don't know what to do

2
To this day
your sad lullaby, Mama,
echoes in my ears
like caravan bells
To this day
the taste of your bitter labor
is still under my ungracious tongue
I was born into this world
bearing your wishes on my shoulders
Did I feel this way in the cradle
as my mouth tightened around your nipple?
I am your son, Mama, your son
who grew up counting the stars

وحيدك أنا يا أماه ، وحيدك...

الذي ترعرع يعد النجوم

ومع وابل المطر الأول

اندفعت إلى الشارع

صفقتُ بيديّ مع أوراق الشجر

غنيتُ مع الرياح

ذات يوم

لم أعد مرئياً لعينيك في الحي

لقد تهتُ مع شرودي

على دروب الترحال

لأول مرة صادفت الجبال

وحين رأيت الذرى المغطاة بالثلوج

تخيلت شيب جدي

كما تلتْ عليّ الغابات كتبَ الخريف

والطيور التي هاجرتْ

إلى ربيع الإنسان

وحاورتني طويلاً

غيمات ليس لها مأوى

وأنا أصفي إلى صمتها المثقل بقصائد البرق

مسنداً رأسي إلى جذع الصفصاف

أنصتُ إلى ما روى لي النهر

هكذا اعتدت أن أتأمل النجوم

وبالشرود نفسه

مررت ليلاً بقبور أسلافي

حيث يرقدون في ظلمة السماء كالنيازك

ها أنا ذا راحل يا أماه

مهدهداً في فمي غناءك الحزين

حين يهدّ روحي التعب

I rushed into the street
during the first rain shower
I applauded with the leaves
I sang with the wind
One day
you no longer saw me in the neighborhood
as I wandered aimlessly
along unknown paths
The first time I met the mountains
and saw their snow-capped peaks
I imagined Grandfather's white hair
The forests also read me the books of autumn
Birds migrated to the stream of human existence
Clouds without shelter spoke to me
as I listened to their silence
besieged by the lightning of poetry
I listened to what the river told me
my back against the trunk of a willow tree
I contemplated the stars
and in the same aimlessness
passed the graves of my predecessors
the dark night full of falling stars
I am leaving, Mama
My mouth murmurs your sad song
When my soul tires
I fall asleep for a little while
resting my head on the branch of a stream
The dreams of the sparrows also visit me

أغفو قليلاً ورأسي على زند الينابيع
كما يزورني حلم العصافير
حالما تلفّني الظلمات
أماه... كيف لك الآن تفسير أحلامي
كما كنت تفعلين!

٣

على خدي
سقطت قطرة ندى صافية
همستُ: لستُ عشباً يا ذاكرة الفجر
تردّدَ ، برهةً ، رجع الصدى:
من أين آتي
لو لم تحن إلى بيتك القديم
ساعةَ تفيق الشمس العتيقة ؟!

٤

يا بيتي المنشود
الذي يحيطه سياج الكلام
كنت أشم أريج الأزهار
التي تتفتح في فنائك الصخري
والتي أبداً لا تعيش الذبول
مذ كان قلبي اليانع يرتوي
من ماء الثديين
كنت أعبر بابك السحري
في حكايا جدتي
ومن عصا جدي الصموت
(كلما خطا على العتبة)
كنت ألمح بريق النجوم

with the darkness
Mama. . . how would you interpret my dreams
today as you once did before?

3
A pure drop of dew
fell onto my cheek
I whispered,
I am not grass, O memory of dawn
In the stillness, the echo replied,
Where would I be
if you didn't long for your home
in the ancient presence of the sun?

4
My faraway home
is surrounded by a fence of words
I can smell the blooms of flowers
that never wilt in your rock garden
My mellow heart drinks from the source of water
I crossed your magic door in Grandmother's tales
and whenever Grandfather stepped across the threshold
from his cane emerged the shimmering stars
that lit up your spacious sky
My faraway home
its roof spans my overcast heart
rain always imminent
One night your figure appeared before me

التي تضيء سماءك الرحبة
يا بيتي المنشود
الذي سقفه قلبي الملبّد
حيث يوشك على الهطول
مرة ، جاءني طيفك ليلاً
حلماً ينوح على وسادتي
ثم غادرت الطفولة قلبي
كما خرجت من بيتنا القديم
في تلك الليلة
وإلى الأبد
كمن يسير في حلمه
حاملاً بين يديه الوسادة...

as if in a dream my tears fell upon the pillow
and then the child vanished from my heart
and I emerged from our old home
that night
and forever after
as one who walks in a dream
holding a pillow. . .

ميتافيزيقا امرأة ثلاثينية

إلى بورخيس وآخرين
- بياتريث بيتربو

لهفتي إلى مضاجعة الغرباء من الرجال
العابرين كصرختي الأنثوية
المتنائين في جسدي
لهفتي إلى أن ألمس برق أجسادهم
الوحشي والمقدس
والذي لا ترقى إليه النساء...
لهفتي هذه تقض مضجعي

جسدي جبل صخري
إذ يعبر الغرباء من الرجال
ويحتمون من قيظ النهار وقسوة الترحال
بكهفه الرطب
حيث يتناءون شهقة ، شهقة
في أغواري المظلمة
وعبر فوضى روحي الرهيبة
يبلغون صرختي

الزمن يستغرق نفسه...
يا غرباء عن حياتي
يا عابرين في جسدي
يا متنائين في صرختي
إني أعلم
أنني في بعض الأحيان
وبالحنين نفسه

Metaphysics of a Woman in Her Thirties

To Borges and others
—Beatriz Viterbo

The lust to make love to strangers
those transient as my scream
those distancing my body
The lust to touch the brutal and holy lightning
of their bodies
the bodies of men I cannot reach. . .
such a troubling, terrifying lust

My body is a mountain of rocks
strangers climb
take shelter from the noon heat
rest upon on their toilsome travels
Inside my moist caves
they further the distances
gasp by gasp in my dark hollows
until they make me scream
with the horror of my soul

Time flows on. . .
O strangers
O transients in my body
O furthering distances
I know, perhaps from nostalgia,
that I've confused the brutal and holy lightning
of your bodies
with the love of my husband and children

أخلط بين برق أجسادكم
الوحشي والمقدس
وبين زوجي وأولادي
الذين أحبهم

صوت الغرباء من الرجال
صادراً من صرختي
يظل يتكلم
أحياناً ، وأنا أقرأ كتباً قد أزحت عنها الغبار
أتلقى رسائلهم
التي تذكّرني كيف أن صرختي
كانت تتفتت في برق أجسادهم
كانت تتناثر في آبار روحي

ضوء الفجر
التائه
ولج سريري البارد كالرخام
حينئذ ، تذكرت صرختي الأنثوية
التي جعلت الرجال
الغرباء عن سريري
العابرين كضوء تائه
المتنائين في الفجر
يتحدثون طوال الليل

مع ذلك ، أرتاب في قدرتهم على امتلاكي
(أولئك الغرباء عن شعوري
أولئك العابرين في كلامي
أولئك المتنائين في غربتي)
لأن ذلك يعني
أنهم تناسوا اختلافي

The voices of the strangers
still echo in my screams
Sometimes
after I wipe the dust off a book
I receive their messages reminding me
of how my screams shattered the lightning
of their bodies and scattered into the wells of my soul

Dawn's stray light
penetrates my marble-cold bed
and again I recall my screams
that made those strangers
as transient as the light
so distant at dawn
talk through the night

But I doubt
they are capable of receiving me
strangers to my feelings
ignorant of my words
furthering my isolation
for they disregarded my otherness
as I, too, became lust generalized
a quick pleasure

I imagined those men
in their terrible isolation
their holy journey
their furthering distances
tamed by my screams

يعني تعميمي
يعني عهري

واعتدت ، أيضاً ، أن أتخيل الرجال
(أعني غربتهم الرهيبة
عبورهم القدسي
تنائيهم في اللا نهائي)
الذين تهزهم صرختي الأنثوية
وتجعلهم أليفين

صوب الغرباء من الرجال
هناك ، حيث صرخات جديدة لجسدي
أجهلها
أتخيلها غريبة ، عابرة ، متنائية
في برق أجسادهم
في ذلك الاتجاه
أولي وجهي راقدة في سريري
كي أنام

أنا الآن في الثالثة والثلاثين من عمري
إذ ولدت في قرية سومرية
بدت لهم صرختي الأنثوية
أثرية كالفخار
أكثر قدماً من سومر
سابقة على غربة الرجال
أفكر في أن كل صرخة من صرخاتي
ستدوم في ذاكرتهم
كما أن حنيني إلى برق أجساد الرجال
الذي يضيء غربتي
لا يني يقض مضجعي

As I fall asleep
and turn my gaze toward
future strangers
new screams rise within me
strange, transient, distant
in the lightning of their bodies

I, Beatriz, am in my thirty-third year
and was born in a Sumerian village
My screams seemed to them
an archaeological find
a potshard older than Sumer
dating before their isolation
I think each scream of mine
will survive their memories
And my nostalgia
for the lightning of their bodies
still illuminates my isolation
in terrifying lust

ئۆندا تورۇس ۋە زامان شەكىللەنمەكتە

I

كۆن چىققاندا بوسۇۋقتىكى قوچقاجتەك
يىقىنلاشتى زۇۋۇانىمغا سۆكۈنات ،
گويا قانات قىقىلىشىدەك...

قاراگمۇلۇق ھەمدە يىلان ئۆندە
ئۆرتەنگەن كۆل ئۈستىدە ئاي نۆرىدەك .

ماگا ئوخشاش
بۇلۇتلاردا ئۆچكەن شەپەق ئەسلىمىسىدەك ،
چوقىلاردا روھ يالقۇنىدەك...

شۆندا قلا تەن يورۇماقتا بۇ يەردە .

2

خەيرلىك ئاخشام ، ئەي چىبكەتكىلەر !
ئەي چىمىلقلار ، خەيرلىك ئاخشام!
بىزگە تالىق بۇ نۇرلۇق ئاي
ئالقىنىمنى نۇرغا يۇمغان بۇ جايدا .

چىمىلقلاردا ئوگدا ياتقانچە ،
چىبكەتكىلەر ئاۋازىغا ئورۇنۇپ ،
تارىلىمەن ئۆزۈمگە شۇدەم
بۇ ئايدىڭدا دەرەخلەرنىڭ سايىلىرىدەك .
ئۆزۈمگە يات ،
سۆزلەرگە يات ھالەتتە .
ھەم ئوي-پىكرىم كېزەر نىگاھ يىراقلىقىدا
كۆزۈمدىكى كۆمۈشنىڭ يالتىرىشىدەك ،
سۆكۈناتنىڭ قاتلاملىرىدا .

Where Ceiling and Time Form

1

Like a bird at dawn's threshold
silence approaches my tongue
a flutter of wings
Like spilled moonlight on a lake
shimmers in the darkness
the hiss of a snake
I remember
twilight in the clouds
the flame of the soul on the peaks
while here, a body glows

2

Good evening grasshoppers!
Good evening meadow!
The bright moon shines for us
shines into my closed palms
Lying on the meadow
under the shadows of trees
the grasshopper chatter spreads through me
This moonlit night
I am a stranger to myself
and to other voices
My thoughts wander along the sightline
glittering silver in my eyes
into the caverns of silence

3

ياشىماقتمەن ياشاۋاتقاندەك
مەن ياشنغان بۇ يەردە.

سۆيىمەن ناننى شاراپ سۆيگەندەك ،
ھارغىنلىقنى سۆيىمەن ھەم ھاردۇق سۆيگەندەك ،
نامراتنمۇ سۆيىمەن باينى سۆيگەندەك ،
ياخشىلىقنى سۆيىمەن ھەم يامانلىقنى سۆيگەندەك.

بىراق ،
سۆكۈناتنىڭ شىرىلدىشىنى قىلمەن تەقىب ،
ھەر دەققە ، ھەر يەردە ،
گويا بوغدا چوققىسىدا ئولتۇرغان ،
گۆركرەشكە ھازىرلانغان شامالدەك.

4

بالداق-بالداق ئۆزلەيمەن پەلەمپەيدىن ئىسككە...

باسقىنىمدا قوڭغۇراقنىڭ كونۇپكىسىنى ،
جاراڭلايدۇ ئايالىمنىڭ تەبەسسۇمى ،
قىزلىرىمنىڭ شادلىقى ،
قولۇمدىكى پۇشۇرۇلغان توخۇ ئاۋازى ،
قەلبىمدىكى پەۋەس خۇشاللىق...

شۇ ۋاقىتنىڭ ئۆزىدە يەنە
ئاگلايمەن يىراقلاردىن سۆكۈناتنىڭ جاراڭلىشىنى -
ئىچ-ئىچىمدىن ئاستا-ئاستا ئۆرلىگەن.

112

3
I live as I've lived wherever I live
I like bread I like wine
I like exhaustion I like comfort
I like the poor I like the rich
I like good I like evil. . .
But I await the slash of silence
from moment to moment
place to place, like the wind
circling the peaks of the Himalayas
set to blow down the mountain slopes

4
Stair by stair I climb up to the door
I press the doorbell
it rings
my wife smiles
my children laugh
the grilled chicken in my hands cries out
the happiness in my heart feels heavy
I can hear
the silence ringing away
ascending, slowly, within me

5

مەن تۈيمەن سۆكۈنات بلەن ،
ھەم قلمەن تەپەككۈر ئۆزۈم ئۈستىدە.

ئننسانني سۆزلمەك نەقەدەر مۈشكۈل!
«تۈغۇلۇلمىز ، ياشاپ ئۆلمىز ،
غايە ئۈچۈن ياكى غايىسىز ،
بارلىق ئۈچۈن يا يوقلۇقنى دەپ...»
دېپسەك نەقەدەر ئاسان-ھە ، بۇ سۆز!
سۆكۈناتنى سۆزلمەك نەقەدەر مۈشكۈل!
«سۆكۈنات دېمەك...» دەپ گەپ يورغىلاتماق
ئاسان نەقەدەر!

6

زۇۋۇان سۆرگەن بولسا مايسلار!
ھايۇاناتلار سۆزلىگەن بولسا!
سۆزلەشنى ئۈشتۈمتۈت سبغىنىش مەندە!

بۇلاق مەنى قىلار ياردار
ئۆزىننىڭ شۇ سۆپسۆزۈك چوڭقۇرلىقدا
سۆكۈت قىلغان تاشلىرى بلەن!

7

لوڭقىسىدا سۆكۈناتنىڭ
سۆلغان ئۈچ تال گۈل.

بىرى تۈگمەس گۈزەللىكدىن
چۈشكۈنلۈككە بولغان گىرىپتار.
چۈشمەككتە يەنە بىرى
بارلىقىننىڭ خۇشپۇرىقىنى.
ئۈچىنجىسى ئىسيانكار
ئۆزىننىڭ مەنسىز رەڭلىرى بلەن.

114

5

I feel silence
and think of myself

How difficult it is to say "human being!"
and so easy to say "we are born ... we live ... we will die"
for a purpose or no purpose
for a truth or no truth
How difficult it is to say "silence"
and so easy to say "silence is ... silence"

6

If plants said
and animals replied
I, too, would want to speak!

The wounding stream with its silent stones
visible through the water depths

7

Three withered roses
in a vase of silence

A rose that weeps for its infinite beauty
A rose that dreams its essence of being
A rose that rebels against its useless colors

8

نېمه ئېدىم ؟

سۇلار ماڭا قىلار ئىشارەت

بۇلاقلارنى ئەسكەرتىپ .

مەن نېمە ؟

پىچىرلايدۇ ماڭا شامالللار

بوشلۇقلارنى .

بولىمەن نېمە ؟

باقار ماڭا تەگرىلەر

سۇغۇق نەزەردە .

سۇلار ،

بۇلاقلار ،

شامالللار ،

بوشلۇقلار ،

تەگرىلەر ...

سۆكۈناتتا ھەممىسى .

9

گاچا ئەمەس بوسۇق زادىلا!

بولمىسا ،

نېمه ئۈچۈن بۇ خىيالچان رۇجەكلەرنىڭ سۇكۇتى ؟

تۇؤرۇكلەرگە قۇرۇلمىدى ئۆيىمىز ،

بوسۇقتۇر ئۇلى ،

مەنبەسىدۇر يوشۇرۇن .

ئۇندا تورۇس ؤە زامان شەكىللەنمەكتە ...

116

8
Who was I?
Water draws me toward the source

Who am I?
Wind reveals the open road to me

Who will I be?
The gods gaze at me with cold stares

Water, source, wind, road, gods. . .
of silence

9
If the threshold isn't mute
then why the silence of disused windows?
Our home isn't built with columns
its pillar is the threshold
a hidden root

where ceiling and time form

10

شۇندۇاق!

ئۇ ئەينى شۇ سۇكۇنات تۇيغۇسىدۇر ،

قالدىم يەنە ئارسالدى بولۇپ مەن

دېڭىز تەكتىدە بىر قارىغۇ ھېكمەتشۇناستەك

ئۇنتۇلغان لەگگەرمىدۇ ؟ ياكى بولمسا

قۇشمىدۇ قاناتلىرى بوشلۇقلارغا ئۇرۇلغان ،

قارىجۇقلىرى قۇملۇقتىكى جۇپ بۇلاق ؟

قەدىمىي كېمە ،

كاپىتاننى قىرغاققا تاشلىغان دېڭىز.

ياكى بولمسا

شۇۋرغانىدىن

قورام تاشلار ئارسىفا پاناھلانغان ئۇرۇق ،

ئۇرۇۋالغان ئۇنى قۇش پىپى.

ئەينە كېڭگمۇ بار سۇكۇناتى ...

ئۇندا تېخىچە

ئەلمىساقنىڭ ئۇممۇجۇكى تۇرار بىزگە تەكەلىپ

فوسفورلۇق تورلىرىننىڭ ئارقىسىدىن.

ئۇ يورۇتار داۋاملىق

ئازاب دەستىدىن

فوسفوردەك ئالجاناپ ھەمدە بتەرەپ

ئۇممۇجۇككەلەرگە ئايلانغان ھەم زامان شورى ئۇرلىگەن

ئېپادسىز يۈزلىرىمىزنى.

تۇن نىسبىدە ،

تىمىسقىلاپ ئەرۋاھلار چىقىشىدۇ ئەينەكتىن ،

جۇش كەينىدىن جۇش بولۇپ.

10
Yes!
The relentless silence confuses me
an anchor forgotten at the bottom of the sea
a blind sage
Bird wings interrupt the scene
irises like pools in the desert
An ancient ship captain washed ashore
a seed sheltered between rocks in the bitter cold
covered with bird feathers

11
The mirror's silence
in the abyss
where the spider still stares at us
from its phosphorous web that illuminates
the featureless faces of the poets
suffering in indifference
spiders covered with the moss of time

At midnight
ghosts sneak out of the mirror
dream after dream

12

بىر دەمدىن كېيىن ،

ئايدىن كېيىن ، قۇياشتىن كېيىن ،

ھەمدە ساما يولدىن كېيىن...

تۇرار زېمىن

چۆشلىرىمىزدە ئايدىڭگالاشقان ئۇيقۇسىدىن ،

ئاجار ، داغدام ، سۆكۈناتنىڭ دەرۋازىسىنى.

ئاسمانغا ئۇ بېغىشلار ئىسىم:

ئادەملەر بورنى!

زېمىنىمىز ،

ئازابىمىزغا قەدىردان زېمىنىمىز.

12
Shortly thereafter
after the moon, after the sun, after the nebula
earth will rise from its sleep
lit by the moon in our dreams
and a vast silence will open out
to give the sky its name:
Human Hurricane!
Our earth. . .
our earth so dear to our pain

وحشة بيضاء

وحشة بيضاء
فيَّ أنا هذه المعجزة الدائمة...
وهبتها نفسي بحزن وخشوع
كما كان يفعل دونْ جُوان
ضد ديمومة الحنين البشري
يا لها من وحشة خفيفة كالنسيم
يا لها من وحشة رهيبة
كانحلال في دمي
في أعماقي شيء وحيد:
يحتدم اللا شيء

يا لوحشتي البيضاء
يا لذاكرتي السحيقة
يا لجنتي في الجحيم
جثة فرعون
برج بابل
الأهرام
أعمدة اليونان
ناطحات السحاب في نيويورك...
كلها ألوان يمحوها بياض الوحشة

يا للوحشة البيضاء
يا لقلب ينبض للكون
يا لصمت الشعراء
يا لصفر الرياضيات الجليل
قد التقيتُ بالآلهة التائهين
الساكنين كهوف الوحشة

White Loneliness

White loneliness
a permanent miracle within me
I've created it myself in grief and devotion
as Don Juan created his loneliness
against human desire
A light loneliness like a breeze
A terrible loneliness like bloodletting
Only one thing left for me:
nothingness

O my white loneliness
O my timeless memory
O my heaven in hell
Pharaoh's body
the Tower of Babel
the pyramids
a Greek column
a Manhattan skyscraper...
colors erased by the whiteness

O white loneliness
O the beating heart of the universe
O the silence of poets
O the dignified zero of mathematics
I have met the wandering gods
who dwell in the caves of loneliness
for whom the sun eternally repeats itself

والشمس تعيد ذاتها على الدوام

من أجلهم

أنا الذي رأيتُ بروقَ الوحشة

حتى في عيون الأطفال

كما تخيلتُ وحشتي البيضاء

كفناً مقدساً يلفّ الموتى

I see the mark of loneliness
even in the eyes of children
I imagine my white loneliness
is a holy shroud for the dead

حصتي من الليل

from

My Share of the Night

(2007)

ئەي ، كىچە

ئەي كىچە ، ئۆتۈپ كەتكىنى كىچەگكەن
ئۆتۈپ كەتكىنى كىلدىفىننكەن
گۇناھكار ناخشام
يۇكسەكلىرىگدىن ئاقار يۇلتۇزدەك چۈشۈپ كېتىۋاتىدۇ
چىچىلاگفۇ تەشۈشىم
تىرەنلىرىگدە قاريغۇ يىللانلاردەك قۇتراۋاتىدۇ

ئەي كىچە ، ئۆتۈپ كەتكىنى كۆلەگگەگكەن
ئۆتۈپ كەتكىنى كىلدىفىننكەن
ئۇندا ، تاگدىن تاگغا پۇتلىشسىپ كېتىۋاتىمەن
ئۇلار سەندىن چۈشۈپ قالغان كۆلدۈرمىلار
ئۇندا ، بۇرۇتى خەت تارتقان چۈشۈم
قۇياشنىڭ ئەمچەكلىرىنى سىلاپ ئۆلۈپ قىلىۋاتىدۇ

ئەي كىچە ، ئۆتۈپ كەتكىنى قۇياشىگگەن
ئۆتۈپ كەتكىنى كىلدىفىننكەن
مەن ئۇنىڭ مەگگۈلۈكۈگدىكى پەرىشان ئاشىقى
ئۇلۇممىدىن تەگرىدەك قوپۇپ
شەپەقنىڭ ئارقا تەرىپىدىكى پاسق كارۇتىدا
ئارام تاپقان شۇ قۇياشنىڭ زاۋاللىقىنى ئۈنسىز كۈيلەيمەن

ئەي كىچە ، ئۆتۈپ كەتكىنى كىچەگكەن
ئۆتۈپ كەتكىنى كىلدىفىننكەن
ئۇندا
يەنىلا
سىننڭ ئاقار يۇلتۇزدەك ئۆتكۈنچى
ھەم شەپەقتەك زاۋال تايقۇچى نقابىك بولۇپ قىلىۋېرىمەن

O Night

What passed was your night
O night, what passed was upcoming
This is my ancient ode
falling as a star from your infinite heights
this is my rebellious soul
climbing from your depths like a blind snake

What passed was your shadow
O night, what passed was upcoming
I walk, tripping my way across your steps
dawn
after dawn
the dust-covered copper bells
of my young dream die, as I
hold the budding warmth of the sun

What passed was your sun
O night, what passed was upcoming
I am here, her sad lover, in your eternity
I rise
from my death like a god
and quietly sing her long descent
while she hides in twilight delight
as if ensnared by a dark sin

What passed was your night
O night, what passed was upcoming
I am still here and will stay—
your fleeting mask like a falling star
your ephemeral one like the twilight

الثانية عشرة

يا لتلك النباتات الكثيفة
تنمو ، تتسلق صمتي هناك
قال وهو يرمق الساعة الجدارية
تشير عقاربها إلى الثانية عشرة ليلاً

ثم تناول من على الرفوف
كتاباً عتيقاً يعلوه الغبار
كذرات ضوء شعشعت دهراً
وقد عتمت لتو

فكّر ، برهةً ، برياح موسمية هوجاء
ما فتئت تعصف بمنازلنا المتداعية
على مشارف الفجر
وأجنحة الطير الوافد من أقاليم
لم تطأها أقدام أبالسة النور وملائكة الظلام
كانت تلطم أجفاننا المطبقة
على سراب يدنو
من عتباتنا المغمورة بالرمال...

كانت عقارب الساعة الجدارية
تشير إلى الثانية عشرة ليلاً

تنهّد هامساً:
وكمثل ذئاب شاردات ، أيها الشعراء
عندما نعوي طويلاً قمرَ منتصف الليل
كانت الشمس ترتكب مصيرها المعهود
في سماء حاستنا اللغوية
ذلك الحدث الضارب في العبث

Midnight

"The plants that have fed off my silence
are overgrown," he said to the clock
on the wall that pointed to midnight

From the shelves he chose
an ancient book covered with dust
particles of light through the ages
now extinguished

He was reminded of the seasonal winds
ravaging the shanty residences
on the outskirts of dawn
where the demons of light and the angels of darkness
never visited
but the wings of birds
flutter against closed eyes
envisioning a mirage
that nears the threshold filled with sand. . .

The wall clock points to midnight

He whispers forlornly,
"Like wandering wolves, O poets,
howling at the midnight moon
the sun accorded its usual fate
in the sky of our language
the utter futility

ولطالما تكرّر منذ قديم الزمن
ولطالما شهده البشر مرة تلو الأخرى
كما سيشهدونه عما قريب
في الظهيرة

كانت عقارب الساعة الجدارية
تشير إلى المخطوط العتيق
يففو بين يديّ

How often it recurs, since the beginning of time
and how often we have witnessed it
over and over and will see it soon
again at noon"

The wall clock points to the ancient book
that sleeps in my hands

حصتي من الليل

عابراً كما النيزك ، زائلاً كالشفق...
وهذا العالم العتيق العتيق
كما لو أنه تبغ معتق
أشق زاوية السماء
وألفّه بها
أنا الأليف الغريب
المأخوذ بتبغه أكثر من الموت

أسير في شوارع أتخيلها
حيث القصائد تتساقط من فمي الخريفيّ
مع نثار التبغ
تلتقطها النجوم بأياديها النحيلة
ذات حصة لي من الليل
هي حياتي كلها
هي موتي كله

My Share of the Night

Ephemeral as a falling star, evanescent as twilight
and this old, old world
is like mellow tobacco. . .
I rip off a corner of the sky and roll it up
I, the most familiar the most strange
more concerned with tobacco than death

I walk along the streets of my imagination
poems falling from my autumn mouth
with flecks of tobacco
The starlight picks them up with slender fingers
the whole of my life
the whole of my death
my share of the night

شەھەرنزادنىڭ ئاغزىدىن ئۆزلۈكسىز ئۆتمۆاتقان كېچىلەر

مەن ئولتۇرۇپ ئادەتلەنگەن
بىر ئاممۇپى باغچىدىكى
دەرەخ شاخلىرىنىڭ قويۇق سايىسى ئاستىدا
كۆندۆزدىن ئاز-تولا بەھرىمان بولغاچ
ۋە سەيلە قىلغۇچىلارنىڭ يۈزىدىكى قۇياشنى
ھەمدە ئاسپىلت يېرىقلىرىدىن جىملارنىڭ ئۈنۈشىنى كۆزەتكە چ
شەھەرنزادنىڭ ئاغزىدىن ئۆزلۈكسىز ئۆتۆۋاتقان كېچىلەرنىڭ مابەينىدە
يۈز بېرىۋاتقان قەتلە قىلىشنىڭ ئەھمىيىتى ھەققىدە ئويلىنىۋاتقانىمدا
ھاياتىمنىڭ قاراڭغۇ ئەينەكلىرىدىن
تەقدىرىمنى ئايدىڭلاشتۇرۇپ بېرىش ئۈچۈن
مەندىن رۇخسەت سوراپ
بىر پالچى ئايال ئالدىمغا كەلدى

سۆكۈت ئىچىدە
ئۇنىڭ ھېلىگەر كۆزلىرىگە تىكىلگەنچە
ئۆزۈن ۋاقىت خىيالغا پاتتىم بولغاي
قارسام
شەھەرنزاتنىڭ ئاغزىدىن ئۆزلۈكسىز ئۆتۆۋاتقان كېچىلەردەك
قەدەملىرىنى تېزلەتىپ مەندىن ئۇزاقلاشتى
بۇ قەدەملەر
گوياكى سەيلە قىلغۇچىلارنىڭ بويىنغا ئېسىلغان قوڭغۇراقلاردەك
ئاگۇلانمىغۇدەك ئاۋازدا ياڭرايتتى
بۇ قەدەملەر
گوياكى جىملارنىڭ ئۈنۈشىنى قۇتلاۋاتقاندەك
ئاسپىلت يېرىقلىرىدىن
كۆرۈنمىگۆدەك نۇرلار بىلەن پارلايتتى

136

Nights that Pass from Scheherazade's Mouth

In a park beneath a shade of trees
as I sat in the presence of the day
watching Ankara's sun on people's faces
and on the grass between the cement cracks
I thought about the possibility of committing murder
in the nights that pass from Scheherazade's mouth
A fortune-teller then appeared
and asked permission to clear
the clouded mirrors of my life
and illuminate my fate

For a while my mind went blank
as I stared into her cunning eyes
in shared silence
until I realized she had left
her steps quickening farther away
in the nights that pass from Scheherazade's mouth
Her steps rang
with echoes of ancientness
like pendant bells against the chests of wanderers
The unseen light shining
into the cracks of the cement
as if to celebrate whatever growth was there

What I wanted to know
was if she could really determine
the unknown, a human's will

شۇ چاغ

بىز كۈندۈزدىن ئاز-تولا بەھرىمان بولغاچ

كېچىلەرنىڭ ئۇزۇلۇكسىز ئۆتۈشلىرىدىن قۇياشنى كۆزەتكە چ

ھەمدە پارلاق قەدەملىرىمىزدىن جىمىلار ياگرىغان ھالدا

ئاممۇۋي باغچىلاردا سەپىلە قىلىۋاتقاندىن بۇيان

ھەتتاكى ئاللاھ بىلەن شەيتانمۇ بىلىشكە ئاجىزلىق قىلغان

ئىنسانىيەتنىڭ ئىستىكنى ئۇ پالچى ئايالنىڭ بىلىپ — بىلەلمەيدىغانلىقىنى

بىلىشنى خالايتتىم

that which is impossible for even gods and demons
to discern, as we wander leisurely in public parks
in the presence of the day
watching the sun in the nights that pass
our shining steps echoes upon the grass. . .

إحساس غريب بالأشياء الأليفة

تبغ

دم لا ريب فيه...
يقطر من شفتين مطبقتين على شوك الأسرار
يقطر...
على كف ينعق عليه الغراب

قبعة

يوم الحداد على خيول تسبل على العيون
كالأجفان...
تصعد الأحجار ضباباً
وهي تشهد على قوارب تنساب من وجوهنا

رقص

ريح التجلي
ترمي الله على التراب
مع صعود الأذان
من مئذنة الجسد

غناء

ثمة جثة
تجرها كاهنات الحب الاثنتا عشرة
إلى سرير مالح
ويتبعهن الموت ككلب شارد

Strange Sense of Familiar Things

Tobacco

Drops of blood
drip from lips closed around a thorn
guarding secrets
drip
onto a palm branch
where a crow caws

Hat

Day of mourning
Warhorses impede the horizon. . .
Stones lift with the fog
reveal the boats that float before us

Dance

The wind of appearances
casts God upon the soil
as *adhan* rises
from within the body's minaret

Song

There, a corpse. . .
Twelve temple priestesses draw it to a salt bed
while death follows
like a wild dog

فستان

على قوس القزح الممتد
من الغرائز حتى شمس الغياب
شاهدتُ عذارى حزني
لا يضاهيهن المطر

كتاب

سمفونية الصمت...
قلعة أسرثُ مارد الروح...
خاتم الينابيع
لسلالة الحجر...

خمر

يا إلهة النسيان!
أنا النديم المثقل بأقمار الذاكرة
تعالي نشرب طوال الليل
بجمجمة ذئب

تنور

من اليورانيوم
تنبت وردتنا المطرودة من المدينة
تلك التي نسيها الرومانس
مع ذهب الكلام

Dress

Beyond the rainbow that stretches
from instinct to the black sun
I saw the young virgins of my sorrow
unmatched by the rain

Book

A symphony of silence. . .
A castle imprisoning the soul-giant. . .
The last spring of water
of the stone dynasty

Wine

O goddess of forgetfulness
I am the one drunk on the moons of memory
Come! Let us drink all night
from the skull of this wolf

Oven

The rose expelled from our village
survives on uranium
What is forgotten in the romance
in the speech of golden tongues

عود

هو حنين بتاج من الشوك
يقود قافلة من النوق
في صحراء الجسد
... أنا وتره الشريد

قلب

قطرة ندى مغلقة على العالم
نجفل
من رعشتها
على عشب زجاجي

Guitar

Nostalgia wears a crown of thorns
and leads a convoy of camels
through the desert of the body. . .
I am its homeless string

Heart

A drop of dew the world enclosed. . .
We are shocked
by its trembling
on a grassblade of glass

ذات قمر ناء في الطفولة

١. حلم

ذات قمر ناء في الطفولة...
كان ثمة حلم
لا يكبر
أصم ، أبكم ، أعمى
يرفرف هناك بملايين الأجنحة
على جبانة أجدادي
التي عرفتُ اسمها لما كبرتُ:
الكرة الأرضية

٢. شقاوة

ذات مساء ناء في الطفولة...
سرقت القمر
وخبأته داخل مقلمتي
استيقظت العتمة العجوز
ثم خرجت إلى الطرقات الخرساء
وهي تنادي بصوتها الباكي:
- يا حفيدي!
أين أنت يا قمري...؟!

٣. تاجر عاديات

ذات صباح ناء في الطفولة...
وأنا أقيس الشمس بالنهار
والنهار بالأحلام
رأيت الليل على الرصيف
يجلس القرفصاء
وأمامه «بسطة» من الأقمار والنجوم

The Moons of Childhood

1. Dream

When the moon floated far from childhood
the dream never grew up
Deaf, dumb, blind
it soared upon millions of wings
toward the graveyard of my ancestors
that as a grownup I only later learned
was called: Earth

2. Mourning

When the moon floated far from childhood
I stole it
and hid it inside my pencil case
The old darkness was awakened
and slipped out to the deaf roads
calling in a mournful voice,
"O my grandson,
where are you, my moon. . . ?"

3. Art Dealer

When the moon floated far from childhood
I measured the sun by days
and the days by dreams

٤. الصياد والسمكة الذهبية

ذات حلم موغل في الطفولة...
كان الليل بحراً مقمراً
والقمر سمكة ذهبية
وكان الأفق يصطادها كل فجر
ثم يعيدها إلى البحر من جديد
كل غسق

٥. حزن

ذات حزن موغل في الطفولة...
كم بكيت
ودمعي تكفكفه أمي
وهي تقهقه بملء شدقيها
وأنا أخبرها كيف أن القمر
اختفى غارقاً في أمواج الغيوم
وأني
كنت أمد كلتي ذراعيَّ
لإنقاذه

٦. بؤبؤ الله

ذات قمر ناء في الطفولة...
كنت جالساً على حافة الشرود
حين وشوش جدي والديّ
بأني جالس في بؤبؤ الله
فلا هم إن كانت عيونه
مفتوحة
أو مغمضة

I saw the night on the sidewalk
sitting cross-legged
in front of a pile of moons and stars
for sale

4. The Fisherman and the Golden Fish

When the moon floated far from childhood
the night became the starry sea
and the moonlight golden fish
The horizon hunted the fish each morning
and returned them to the sea at dusk

5. Sadness

When the moon floated far from childhood
I cried. . .
Mother wiped my tears away with a laugh
as I told her how the moon
started to drown in the waves of clouds
and so I threw out my arms
to save it from vanishing

6. God's Pupil

When the moon floated far from childhood
I was sitting at the edge of nothingness
Grandfather whispered to my parents
that I was sitting in God's pupil
so it didn't matter if His eyes
were open or closed

٧. الإحساس بالليل

ذات حداد موغل في الطفولة...
غفا القمر المتعب
مستلقياً على الغمام
ثم هوى قبيل الفجر إلى الأرض
من فرط الكابوس
حينئذ
استيقظ في قلبي
الإحساس بالليل

٨. الهروب بالأرض

ذات مطر ناء في الطفولة...
حاول جاهداً قوس القزح
أن يحمل الأرض بين ذراعيه
يومها
تساءلت طويلاً:
ترى ، إلى أين كان ينوي
أن يهرب بها ؟!

٩. عقد قران

ذات خاطر موغل في الطفولة...
أسرّ البحر لليابسة
ساعة السحر:
ماذا لو ، عزيزتي ، عقدنا القران
بين القمر السقيم بعمى الألوان
والشمس المصابة
بفقدان الذاكرة ؟

7. Night's Presence

When the moon floated far from childhood
it was so tired that it fell asleep
on a cloud
Long before morning
it had a bad dream
and tumbled to the ground
In that moment
the night's presence
woke my heart

8. Escape with the Earth

When the moon floated far from childhood
the rainbow tried so hard
to carry Earth in its arms
and all day I wondered
where was it planning to escape
with the Earth?!

9. Knot

When the moon floated far from childhood
the sun had barely risen
and the sea said to the land,
"What if, my friend, we tied a knot
between the colorblind moon
and the forgetful sun?"

١٠. تساؤلات ميتافيزيقية

ذات غسق ناء في الطفولة...
استلقت الريح على السطح
بجانبي...
كانت غارقة في التفكير:
أين ابتدأتُ ؟
أين ستنتهي ؟
ماذا تريد؟...

١١. تدريب لغوي

ذات درب ناء في الطفولة...
كان القمر يسند قامتي
كلما سقطت على الليل
كما كانت تسندني الشمس
كلما تعثرتُ بالنهار

١٢. نافذة صغيرة

ذات ربيع ناء في الطفولة...
كان لي نافذة صغيرة
كنت أشاهد منها في الصباح
حلماً غادرني في الليل
مرة
لمحت أبي عائداً من الحرب
متدثراً بنعشه
فتحطمت آنذاك
نافذتي الصغيرة

10. Metaphysical Questions

When the moon floated far from childhood
the wind rested on the roof
beside me, whispering:
Where did it begin?
Where will it end?
What does it want?

11. Language Practice

When the moon floated far from childhood
I tripped over the night
but the moon still pulled me back
the same way the sun held me up
whenever I stumbled over the day

12. Small Window

When the moon floated far from childhood
through a small window I watched
a dream leave the night behind
It was morning
and I saw my father
back from the war
lying in a pool of his own blood
Then my small window shattered

١٣. انتظار

ذات فرح موغل في الطفولة...
أردت أن ألملم النجوم
من السماء
لكم بقيت ليلتها منتظراً
فما كان يغمض القمر جفنيه
ويغفو

١٤. كلام مقمر

ذات خوف موغل في الطفولة...
اختفى القمر
وكانت النجوم ترتعد في الظلام
صعد قلبي أعالي السماء
فكانت حصتي من الليل
أكثر إقماراً

13. Waiting

When the moon floated far from childhood
I wanted to pluck the stars from the sky
I stayed up all night waiting
and the moon never shut its eyes to sleep

14. Moonlit Speech

When the moon floated far from childhood
it vanished—
The stars trembled in the darkness
My heart climbed high into the sky
so that my share of the night
reflected its silver light

بۇلاق ئاستا ئويغىتىدۇ چىملارنى

ئاسماندا ئاي سارغايغان شۇنچە ...
بۇلاقتىكى ئاي ،
چۈشلىرىنى يىغار چېچە كىنك
ھاۋادا توزغان نەي ى مۇردسسدىن .

بۇلاق ئاستا ئويغىتىدۇ چىملارنى ،
بىر رىۋايەت كەلدى ئېسىمگە:
كىرگەنمىش ئاي تۈيىغۇ بىغىغا ،
قاپتۇ شۇ دەم بوغۇزلانغان توزغا ئايلىنىپ .

ئاي شولسىسى جىمقىقاندا كۆزۈمدە ...
بۇلاقتا غايىپ بولۇپ كېچە يەلكىنى ،
يۇلتۇزلارغا ئايلىنار تەنلەر ،
گۇناھ — بايرامفا .

ئاي يۈيدۇ نۇردا بۇلاق ئېسىنى ،
بۇلاق —
تۈننىك يۆكسەكلىرىدىن
ئۆركەشلگەن ئاي .

A Stream Gently Wakens the Young Grass

The moon, so pale in the sky,
threads a garland of flowers in a stream
a garland linked by the poets whose spirits
fly through the air

A stream gently wakens the young grass
recalling the night when the moon
entered the garden of knowledge
and recognizing death turned into a peacock

When the moon's shadow falls into the eyes
the night procession vanishes in the stream
bodies transform into stars
and sin turns into a holiday

The moon feeds the stream's desires in darkness
for the stream is a moon
that rushes down
from the heights of the night

ما تبقى من الليل

إنانا...
يا داعرة يحملها ألف سرير وسرير
أنا زوجك المنفي دموزي
أقيم هنا
حيث لا سلطان لشرائع البشر
أعلو وأهبط كمثل بحر
يشكل الموت والحياة
مدي وجزري الأبديين

أكتب إليك الآن من العالم السفلي
طليق الكلام
أسيرَ الليل
أسوق الكلمات
التي تسرح على بياض الورق
لا المواشي
كما كنت أفعل في سالف الأزمان
عندما كان ينبت العشب من الأرض
ويزهر الفكر أملاً أحمر

لي رفض لا يقبل الجدل
فيما يخص تاريخ النهار
منذ نشأته المشبوهة على شكل مسار طاغ
لي ما تبقى من الليل
إذ هو الليل كله
من أول شرود للشمس
وهي تعبر عنق النهار
إلى آخر الأقمار التي أطلقها الأسلاف

What Remains of the Night

Inanna. . .
O courtesan who passed through a thousand and one beds
I, Dumuzid, your exiled husband
reside here with no authority over the human race
I rise and fall like the sea
on the eternal tides
of life and death

I write to you from the world below
unable to speak to you
a prisoner of the darkness
guiding these words across
a blank sheet
instead of the flock
that I watched over so long ago
when grass grew from the earth
and thoughts were like red blooms

I do not believe
in the history of the day
that manipulates by means of force
to form an oppressive path
What remains of the night
is in truth the whole of the night
from the first sun swallowed
by the day
to the last of the moons shot down by the ancestors

كالحسرات
والتي توقظ الذاكرة السقيمة
كطرقات مضطربة
على بوابة العالم السفلي

إنانا...
عندما ألفظ اسمك الشهي
أقصد كل قارئ ينافق المعنى
إذ يصيح مندهشاً وبأعلى صوته
وهو يقرأ ما أكتبه ، أنا الأويفوري
بالعربية الفصحى:
«كلامك ، سيدي ، عرس اللغة
بحضور جميع الآلهة المبتهجين
وغيابِ العريس الذي هو أنت
حيث كالميت تغوص في الأريكة
تلفك سحابة التبغ كالكفن
وقد فرغتَ للتو من الكتابة...»

«أيها القارئ المنافق ، يا شبيهي!»
عندما أقول «ما تبقى من الليل»
أعني ما لنا من حلم يائس
لا تني تنسجه عناكب اللغة
أعني نحن العناكب السود شبيهي دموزي
حيث نروي أنباء العالم السفلي
للأحياء الذين أنكروا الموت
أقول «نروي» وأنا أتهم كلاً منا
فقد تورطنا في مؤامرة غير عادلة
لقتل المنشدين

هكذا غدا ليلنا

like sighs rousing a sickened memory
like troubled knocks on the door of the underworld

Inanna. . .
when I speak your delightful name
I address those hypocrite readers
who shout at me in astonishment
at what I, the Uyghur, write in fluent Arabic,
"Your words, dear sir, are a wedding of language
in the presence of the rejoicing gods
and you, the absent groom,
finished with your writing, sink
into a sofa like a dead man
a cloud of cigarette smoke
enveloping you like a shroud"

Dear hypocrite reader, my friend!
By "what remains of the night"
I mean the desperate dream we possess
and the language spiders weave
and we, the black spiders, multitudes of Dumuzid
we tell the story of the world below
to the ones alive in death's refusal
I write "we tell" to accuse all of us
who take part in the injustice
of killing the poet-singers

- ما تبقى لنا من الليل -

مختل الظلام

فلن تعود حشرجاتنا اللغوية

مزهوة كما كانت

بضوء القمر

Our night becoming
for us what remains of the night
troubled by the darkness
and our echoing tongues no longer
filled by the moonlight
as our words once were

AHMATJAN OSMAN writes in both Uyghur and Arabic, and has also translated the work of numerous poets into Uyghur, including Octavio Paz, Paul Celan, Fernando Pessoa, and Adonis. He is recognized as one of the founders and leading lights of the New Poetry movement that emerged in Uyghur literature in the 1980s. His own literary influ

ences range from modernists like Paul Celan and the Syrian poet Adonis to classical Uyghur authors like the eighteenth-century Sufi poet Meshrep. He is the author of eight collections of poetry, published in Syria and East Turkistan.

JEFFREY YANG is the author of the poetry collections *Vanishing-Line* and *An Aquarium*. He is the translator of Liu Xiaobo's *June Fourth Elegies* and Su Shi's *East Slope*, and the editor of *Birds, Beasts, and Seas: Nature Poems from New Directions* and *Time of Grief: Mourning Poems*. Yang works as an editor at New Directions Publishing and New York Review Books.